WHSmith

Challenge

Science

KS3: Year 8

Age 12–13

Mark Edwards

Introduction

One of the most powerful things about science is its ability to explain many different things using just a few ideas. This book challenges you to use your scientific knowledge to explore all sorts of different situations. The questions are not only designed to give you a thorough revision of all the topics from the Key Stage 3 National Curriculum but also to extend your knowledge and understanding and to get you thinking like a scientist.

Each topic begins with a few practice questions. These introduce you to the ideas and the scientific words that you need to use in the later questions. If you struggle with the practice questions then either move to a new topic or go back to your revision guide (try our *Revise KS3* series). The 'challenge' questions range in difficulty. Some are standard questions that you might see in an exam. Others encourage you to look up further information. A few are designed to really stretch your mind. Don't worry: if all else fails, there are detailed answers at the back of the book. Good luck!

First published 2007
exclusively for WHSmith by
Hodder Education,
an Hachette UK company,
338 Euston Road, London NW1 3BH

Impression number 10 9 8 7 6 5 4 3 2
Year 2011 2010 2009
Text and illustrations © Hodder Education 2007

A CIP record for this book is available from the British Library.

Text: Mark Edwards
Cover illustration: Sally Newton Illustrations

Typeset by Servis Filmsetting Ltd, Stockport, Cheshire

ISBN 978 0 340 94561 2

Printed and bound in Spain.

Contents

1: Food

You will revise:
- the five basic nutrient types
- standard food tests
- what is needed for a balanced diet
- why different people need different diets.

Get started

We need food and water to keep our bodies functioning. But to keep them functioning well, we need a balanced diet appropriate to our lifestyle. We can test different foods to determine what nutrients they provide.

Practice

1 Name the five different nutrient groups.

2 Describe the use that the body makes of each of these groups.

3 What is a balanced diet?

4 Why might different people need different diets?

Challenge

5 An essential chemical that our bodies need is water. The body can survive much longer without food than it can without water.

 a 70% of a child's body mass is water. If their total mass is 50 kg, what mass of water does the child contain?

 b Explain the role of water in the human body in:

  i temperature regulation

  ii transporting chemicals around the body.

 c Suggest why the body can last longer without food than it can without water.

6 **a** What elements are present in carbohydrates other than oxygen?

 b If all the different types of carbohydrates contain the same elements as each other, how are they different?

 c Fibre, starch and sugar are different types of carbohydrate. Name a food source containing each type.

 d Fibre isn't digested by the body. What is it used for?

 e What is the main use of sugars and starch in the body?

7 **a** Explain the difference between proteins and amino acids.

 b State two uses of proteins in the body.

c Name four types of food that are good sources of protein.

d Why must vegetarians be particularly careful about the amount of protein in their diet?

8 Copy and complete this table about the different food tests.

Substance under test	Description	Outcome if substance is present
Starch	**a**	Solution turns blue/black
b	Add a few drops of Benedict's solution to the food solution. Heat test tube in a water bath until the solution boils.	Solution turns orange
Protein	**c**	Solution turns purple
d	Add some ethanol to the food solution and mix well. Then add water to solution and shake again.	Solution turns white

9 Here is some data about two different types of food.

Type of food	Protein (per 100 g)	Carbohydrate (per 100 g)	Fat (per 100 g)
A	23.8	0.0	1.0
B	13.2	65.6	2.0

a One of these types is pasta and the other is chicken. Which is which?

b Suggest why you couldn't live on these food types alone.

c Each of these food types could make up a large proportion of a balanced diet. Give an example of someone who would use type A and an example of someone who would use type B. Explain your answer.

10 Here are some diseases caused by a lack of vitamins or minerals in the body. For each disease, write down the main symptoms of the disease and the mineral or vitamin that is deficient.

a Anaemia   **b** Rickets

c Beriberi   **d** Scurvy

How did I do?

I can list the five nutrient types and explain their role in the human body. ☐

I can describe tests for starch, sugar, protein and fat. ☐

I can suggest a balanced diet for a marathon runner and a pregnant woman. ☐

2: Digestion

You will revise:
- the main parts of the human digestive system
- why we need enzymes
- the right conditions for enzymes to work effectively.

Get started

Once food has entered our bodies, we extract the nutrients we need for short-term and long-term use and excrete or egest the rest.
This process is called *digestion*.

Practice

1 In terms of particles, what is the main function of digestion?

2 State three functions that are performed when humans chew their food.

3 What do we call the chemicals that speed up the process of digestion? What are they made from?

4 Why does the inside of the stomach have to be acidic?

Challenge

5 Here are three types of teeth. For each type explain how they are used to break up the food.

    a Incisors   **b** Canines   **c** Molars.

6 **a** Label this diagram.

    b Explain why we call the digestive system a *system*.

    c The food doesn't pass through some of the organs you have labelled. Which organs are these?

    d In terms of the food passing through the alimentary canal, what are these organs used for?

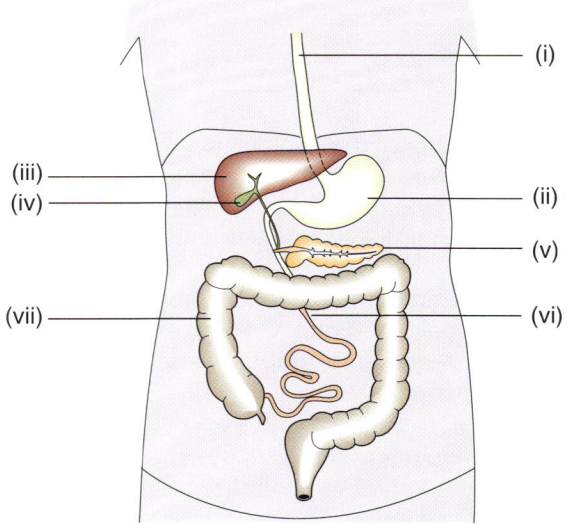

7 **a** Which enzyme does the stomach produce?

b How does the stomach kill bacteria?

c How does the stomach churn the food? What is the purpose of this churning?

d Why does the stomach need a thick inner wall of mucus?

8 **a** Why are alkaline juices added to the small intestine?

b State two functions the small intestine performs to aid digestion.

c The inner wall of the small intestine is covered with little 'finger-like' structures called *villi*. How does this help digestion?

9 **a** State two functions of the large intestine.

b What are the main components of faeces?

c Why do the intestines need a large blood supply?

10 Copy and complete this table.

Nutrient	Enzyme used	Where enzyme is added
Starch	**a**	Mouth
Protein	**b**	**c**
d	Lipase	Small intestine

11 **a** What is peristalsis?

b Explain why this means we can digest food upside down and in space.

12 Why does the blood supply from intestines go directly to the liver?

13 Explain the role of bile.

14 Describe the route of a glucose molecule between digestion and respiration.

How did I do?

I can label a diagram of the digestive system. ✔ ☐

I can describe the process of digestion as food passes along the alimentary canal. ☐

I can state the enzymes that digest a particular nutrient and where they are added. ☐

3: Respiration

You will revise:
- the chemical process of respiration
- why respiration is needed in the body
- how the content of exhaled air varies from inhaled air.

Get started

One important use of food is to provide us with energy. Respiration is the process in which chemical reactions in the cells release this energy so that the cells can perform all their other functions.

Practice

1 Why do germinating peas produce heat? Describe an experiment to demonstrate this.

2 Write down the word equation for aerobic respiration.

3 What are the similarities between respiration and burning?

4 Explain the main difference between respiration and burning.

Challenge

5 Copy and complete this symbolic equation for aerobic respiration (make sure that the equation is balanced).

$C_6H_{12}O_6 + 6 \ldots \ldots \rightarrow \ldots \ldots + \ldots \ldots$

What is the biological purpose of this reaction?

6 Here is a diagram showing an experiment to test the content of exhaled air.

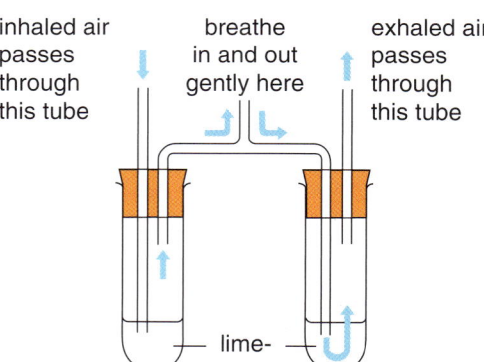

inhaled air passes through this tube

breathe in and out gently here

exhaled air passes through this tube

lime-water

  a What chemical does the apparatus test for?

  b Explain what happens when you breathe gently in and out through the middle tube.

  c How does this show that the chemical must be more concentrated in the exhaled air?

7 What is the other chemical (than the one tested in the apparatus above) that becomes more concentrated in exhaled air? How would you test for it?

8 This table summarises the composition of inhaled and exhaled air.

Substance	Inhaled	Exhaled
Nitrogen	79%	79%
Oxygen	21%	17%
Carbon dioxide	0.04%	4%
Water	1%–1.5%	6%

   a Which substance remains unaffected?

   b Explain why the amount of water in inhaled air can vary.

   c Suggest how the proportion of exhaled water is always the same even though the proportion of inhaled water changes.

   d Where does the extra carbon dioxide come from?

9 You can show that water weed produces carbon dioxide by placing it in hydrogen carbonate solution.

   a Why does the water weed need shielding from light for the experiment to work?

   b State how the solution changes colour during the experiment.

   c Why wouldn't this experiment work with limewater?

   d In order to respire, plants need glucose. Where do they get glucose from?

10 **a** Explain why mammals tend to respire a lot more than reptiles.

   b How do we know that both oxygen and carbon dioxide must dissolve in water?

11 What is anaerobic respiration?

12 Explain how the anaerobic respiration of yeast helps with beer and bread making. Why don't you get drunk eating bread?

13 Explain the benefit of high-altitude training for athletes.

How did I do?

	✔
I can write a word equation and a balanced symbol equation for respiration.	☐
I can explain the main benefit of respiration.	☐
I can describe an experiment to show that organisms respire.	☐
I can analyse the content of inhaled and exhaled air and explain why they are different.	☐

4: Blood circulation and breathing

You will revise:
- how blood is used to transport chemicals around the body
- the direction of blood flow
- evidence for blood circulation.

Get started

In order for our cells to respire, they need a supply of glucose and oxygen. Both breathing and blood circulation ensure that these resources are provided and that the waste products (carbon dioxide and water) are taken away.

Practice

1 Which parts of the blood carry oxygen, glucose, carbon dioxide and water?

2 What is the biological meaning of *inspiration*?

3 Explain the role of the diaphragm in breathing.

4 What are capillaries? Why are they useful?

Challenge

5 Explain why both blood circulation and breathing are needed for successful respiration in the cells.

6 a In the lungs there are about 300 million alveoli. How does the shape of the alveoli contribute to the efficiency of the gas exchange?

   b Suggest why the lining of the alveoli is moist.

   c Describe the direction of movement of gases between the blood and the alveolar duct.

   d Why do the lungs have a very rich blood supply?

7 Here are cross-sections of a vein and an artery.

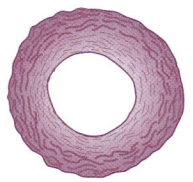 

A   B

   a Which diagram represents an artery and which represents a vein?

   b State one other distinguishing feature that makes veins and arteries different.

   c What is the functional difference between veins and arteries?

   d Explain why an excess of oxygen is usually found in arteries but an excess of carbon dioxide is found in veins.

8 Below is an incomplete schematic diagram of blood circulation.

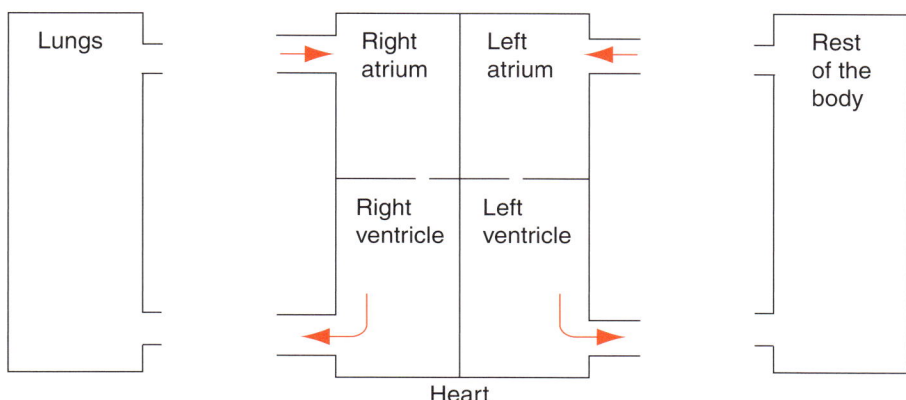

Copy and complete the diagram to show how blood circulates around the body.

9 In 1628 William Harvey published his theories on blood circulation. Here is some of the evidence that he used.

> A The amount of blood going through the heart in an hour is about three times the weight of an average man.
> B Veins have valves in them.
> C Tying valves tightly makes them swell on the side not connected to the heart.
> D Tying arteries tightly makes them swell on the side connected to the heart.

a Which piece of evidence suggests that the blood circulates around the body rather than being made by the heart and then destroyed?

b What can be deduced from fact B?

c How do facts C and D demonstrate the direction of blood flow?

d Harvey experimented on animals. Were these animals alive or dead during the experiments? Explain your answer.

10 Suggest why blood flows much slower in capillaries than it does in arteries.

11 Explain the role of haemoglobin in transporting oxygen.

12 Why is there a vein that carries oxygenated blood? What is its name?

13 What is the role of the kidneys in maintaining a healthy blood supply?

How did I do?

I can describe how blood flows between the heart, the lungs and the rest of the body. ☐

I can distinguish between veins, arteries and capillaries. ☐

I can explain the role of blood circulation in the respiration of cells. ☐

5: Micro-organisms

You will revise:
- bacteria, viruses and fungi
- experimental methods for studying micro-organisms
- how to calculate the size of a bacteria colony.

Get started

There are many different types of micro-organisms that can be investigated in a laboratory. Some of them are useful but some of them are very dangerous.

Practice

1 What is a micro-organism?

2 Explain the main difference between the way bacteria and viruses reproduce.

3 How do fungi reproduce?

4 Many fungi are parasites. What is a parasite?

Challenge

5 **a** Copy and label this diagram of a bacterium.

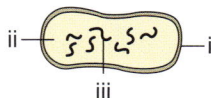

ii ——— i

iii

b What is the main difference between the structure of bacteria and that of animal or plant cells?

c How do bacteria feed?

6 When surgeons carry out operations they have to make sure that their instruments are sterile.

a What is meant by *sterile* in this context?

b What type of radiation do hospitals use to sterilise surgical instruments?

c How can you sterilise instruments in a school science lab?

d Why do you need to sterilise the apparatus before you carry out an experiment using micro-organisms?

e Why do you need to sterilise the apparatus after the experiment?

7 a How does agar jelly promote the growth of a micro-organism colony?

b What other procedure do you use to persuade the microbes to reproduce?

8 a Why did we discover bacteria much earlier than we discovered viruses?

b Explain why you wouldn't be able to grow a virus colony on agar jelly.

c What are the main constituents of a virus?

9 Some bacteria reproduce by splitting into two every 30 minutes.

a If you started with one bacterium, how many would you have after 30 minutes?

b If the population doubles every 30 minutes, how many bacteria will you have after 24 hours?

c Use your answer to part **b** to calculate how many bacteria you would have after 3 days.

d Explain why your bacteria colony is highly unlikely to reach this size.

10 You are carrying out an investigation to see how the amount of carbon dioxide yeast produces depends on the quantity of sugar in bread dough.

a What are the dependent and independent variables in this experiment?

b State two variables that need to be controlled in this experiment.

c How could you measure the volume of carbon dioxide released by the yeast?

d What graph would you plot? What result would you expect to see? Explain your answer.

e Why is bread dough placed in a warm cupboard before it is cooked?

f What type of micro-organism is yeast?

11 Putting food in the fridge makes it last longer before it starts to go off. Why?

12 What is a symbiotic relationship? Describe a symbiotic relationship between bacteria and our bodies.

How did I do?

	✔
I can explain what a micro-organism is and give an example.	☐
I can describe the main parts of a bacterium cell.	☐
I can explain how micro-organisms can be studied safely in the lab.	☐

6: Fighting diseases

Get started

Throughout history we have developed ways to help our bodies fight diseases more effectively. This is a result of gaining an understanding of how diseases are spread and also how the human body naturally defends itself.

Practice

1 What do we call something that causes disease?

2 How are diseases transmitted by vectors?

3 Which micro-organisms can be killed by antibiotics?

4 How do bacteria make us feel ill?

Challenge

5 The human body has several ways to prevent micro-organisms entering it.

   a What is the most obvious barrier to micro-organisms?

   b Explain the function of lysozyme in tears and sweat.

   c Where are the most vulnerable places to infection in the human body?

   d How does mucus help in preventing infections?

   e Explain the purpose of the ciliated epithelial cells lining the air passages to the lungs.

   f How do platelets in the blood help prevent infections?

6 **a** Two main types of white blood cell, phagocytes and lymphocytes, fight infections. What does each type do?

   b How do the white blood cells recognise that the micro-organism is a foreign body?

   c What is an antibody? What is it used for?

   d Explain how somebody can become immune to a particular disease.

7 This diagram shows discs covered in different antibiotics on a plate of agar jelly.

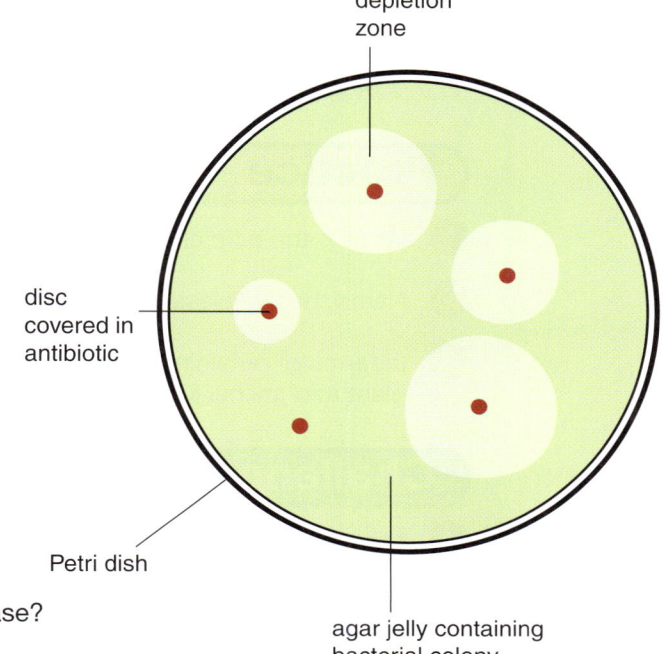

depletion zone

disc covered in antibiotic

Petri dish

agar jelly containing bacterial colony

a Relate how Fleming discovered penicillin using similar apparatus.

b How does the diagram show that some antibiotics kill bacteria?

c Which antibiotic is the most effective in this case?

d Why couldn't this antibiotic be used for all types of bacterial infection?

e Explain why it is important to finish a course of antibiotics even if you are feeling better.

8 **a** Explain why fighting viruses is much harder than fighting bacterial or fungal infections.

b Why are young babies more immune to some viral infections than older children?

c Describe how vaccinations work.

9 What happens in an auto-immune disease?

10 Why are we worried about the overuse of antibiotics?

11 If we become immune to viral diseases once we have them, why can we keep catching colds?

12 Explain the terms *epidemic* and *pandemic*. Why are pandemics far more likely in the modern age?

How did I do?

✔

I can describe five different ways that the body resists or fights infections. ☐

I can explain why antibiotics can be used for certain diseases. ☐

I can explain the role of phagocytes and lymphocytes in fighting infections. ☐

I can explain how the body can become immune to some diseases and the role of vaccinations. ☐

7: Classifying animals and plants

Get started

In order to study habitats effectively it is useful to identify quickly the different species that live in them. A classification system helps you to do this by grouping organisms together that have similar structures.

Practice

1. What is the difference between vertebrates and invertebrates?

2. Name the five classes of vertebrates.

3. In terms of obtaining food, what is the main difference between the plant and animal kingdom?

Challenge

4. Most classification systems start by dividing the different organisms into a small number of groups. Then each group is subdivided into smaller groups, which are then divided further, and so on. Why is this useful to people who want to identify a species quickly?

5. The invertebrates can be split up into about thirty groups. Copy and complete the table summarising some of these groups. You might need to look up some of these in books or on the internet.

Group	Main features	Example
Cnidarians	a	Jellyfish
b	c	Tapeworm
Roundworms	Long, thin, round body	Hookworm
Annelids	d	Earthworm
e	Outer skeleton, jointed legs	Housefly
Echinoderms	f	Starfish
g	Shell (usually) and one 'foot'	Snail

6. a The groups in the table in question 2 can be divided still further. Why is this useful?

   b Explain why some of the groups are divided up into more parts than other groups.

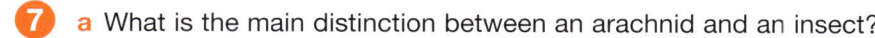

7 **a** What is the main distinction between an arachnid and an insect?

 b To what invertebrate group do these animals belong?

8 Copy and complete this table about the plant kingdom.

Plant group	Leaf type	Spores or seeds?	Roots?
Mosses and liverworts	**a**	Spores	No
Ferns	Fronds	**b**	**c**
d	Needle-like	Seeds	**e**
Flowering plants	Varied	**f**	**g**

9 **a** Why do liverworts need to grow in damp places?

 b Explain how flowering plants and conifers can spread their offspring over a wide habitat much more quickly than the other types of plant. What is the advantage of being able to do this?

10 You are investigating a habitat that contains liverworts, conifers, flowering plants, insects, arachnids and molluscs. Copy and continue this key to help you quickly identify which group an organism belongs to.

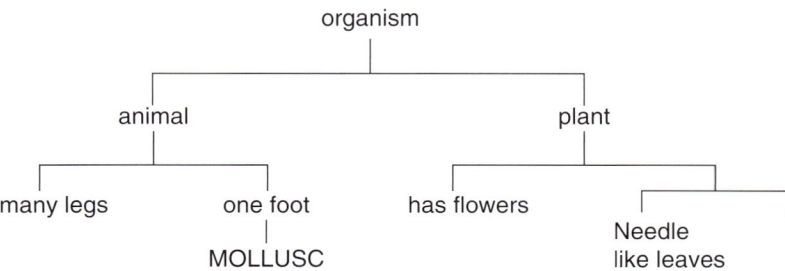

11 Sometimes it is difficult to classify organisms. For example, a squid is a mollusc. Molluscs are characterised as having one foot. What has become of this foot in a squid?

12 Explain why there are far more invertebrate groups than vertebrate groups.

13 Does a sea sponge belong to the animal or the plant kingdom? Explain why it belongs to that kingdom.

How did I do?

I can distinguish between mosses and liverworts, ferns, conifers and flowering plants. ☐

I can describe five classes of vertebrates and seven classes of invertebrates. ☐

I can design a key to help identify a species. ☐

8: Investigating habitats

You will revise:
- methods for obtaining organisms from a habitat
- using transects to study a habitat
- sampling techniques to estimate population size
- analysing populations.

Get started

Ecologists have developed several techniques to help study habitats. These include methods of obtaining organisms to study and ways to estimate the population sizes.

Practice

1 What is sampling? Why do you need it to estimate a population size?

2 How do you make a transect? What is it used for?

3 What is a pyramid of numbers?

Challenge

4 This diagram shows two methods for collecting small animals.

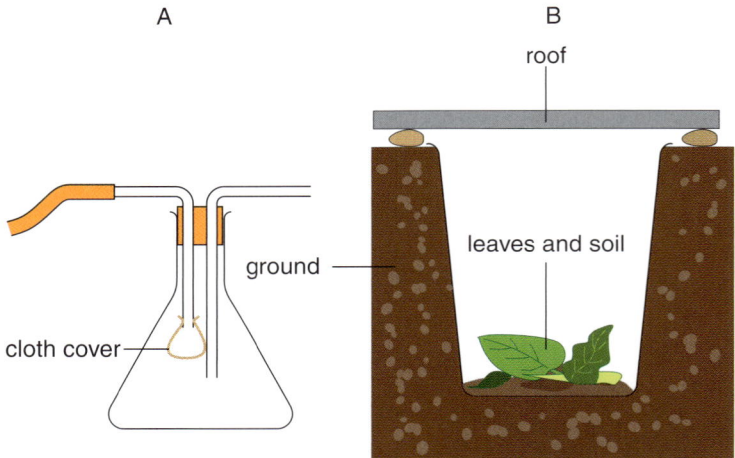

a What is the name of each piece of apparatus?

b Explain why apparatus B might be better at ensuring the sample is completely random.

c State two advantages of using apparatus A rather than B.

5 **a** What is the difference between population size and population density?

b Random sampling of a habitat finds three snails for every 100 square metres. What is the population density of the snails?

c Why are animals likely to be found in clusters rather than evenly spread throughout the habitat?

6 This sketch shows a square metre of habitat using a quadrat.

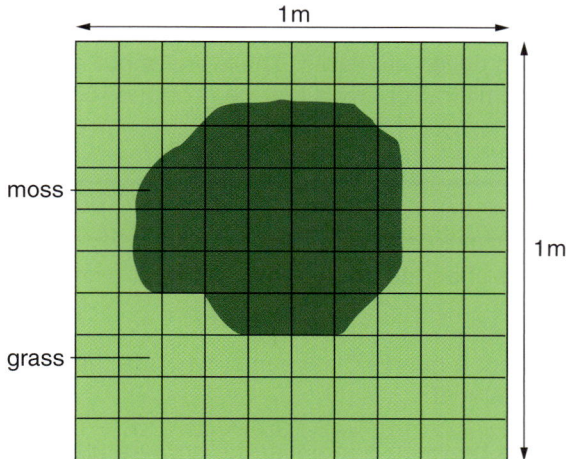

a What sort of animals can be sampled using quadrats?

b Estimate the percentage of grass in this square metre.

c Estimate the percentage of moss.

d Why would it be very difficult to count the number of organisms?

e What would you have to do in order to get a good estimate of the cover of grass and moss in the whole habitat?

7 This graph shows how the populations of foxes and rabbits change with time in a particular habitat.

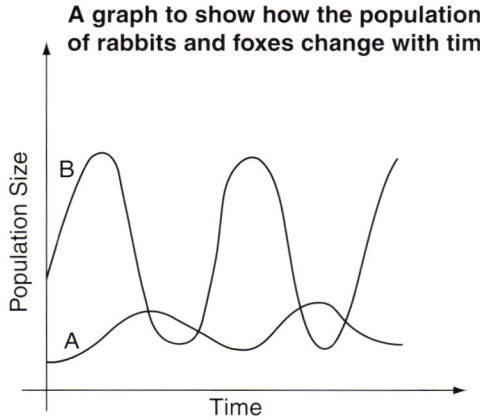

a Which graph represents the fox population? Explain your answer.

b Explain the shape of the graph. Start by assuming the population of the rabbits starts to increase.

9: Atoms and elements

You will revise:
- what is meant by an element
- the symbols and properties of some common elements
- the periodic table.

Get started

All material is made out of particles called atoms. Chemicals made from only one type of atom are called elements. There are about one hundred of them. Elements with similar properties can be grouped together in the periodic table.

Practice

1. Can one element be changed into another element using chemical reactions?

2. If there are only about a hundred elements, why are there so many different types of material?

3. State one difference between a metal and a non-metal.

4. Bromine is a liquid at room temperature; name the only other element that is also in this state.

Challenge

5. Elements are identified by their name (in any particular language) and their symbol.

   a Why is it useful to have a symbol for a particular element?

   b Explain why some symbols have two letters and other symbols have one. Give an example of two elements where this occurs.

   c Why do some elements have a symbol that is not the first one or two letters of their name?

   d Identify these elements from their symbols.

i H	ii Li	iii Ar	iv Na
v K	vi Au	vii Hg	viii Sb

   e Write down the symbols for these elements.

i Helium	ii Calcium	iii Magnesium
iv Chlorine	v Lead	vi Tin

   f Which of the elements in part e are metals and which are non-metals?

6. Three elements are magnetic. Which are they?

7 Here is the first main row of the periodic table.

Li	Be	B	C	N	O	F	Ne

  a Which of these elements are solid and which are gases at room temperature?

  b Identify the two metals and five non-metals.

  c Which element is neither a metal nor a non-metal? What do we call this class of element?

  d Which two of these elements can be found in large quantities in the air?

  e Which element is the main building block for organisms?

  f Why is it rare to find the element fluorine by itself in nature?

8 Here is the first group of the periodic table and some of the characteristics of the elements.

Element	pH of oxide	Behaviour in water	Type of element	Melting point (°C)
Li	alkaline	Bubbles	Reactive metal	181
Na	alkaline	Bubbles vigorously	Reactive metal	98
K	alkaline	Bubbles and catches fire	Reactive metal	63
Rb	alkaline	Vigorously catches fire	Reactive metal	39
Cs	alkaline	Explodes (even reacts with very cold ice)	Reactive metal	28

  a What information suggests that these elements are similar?

  b Explain what happens to the reactivity of the elements as you go down the group.

  c Which elements could possibly be in liquid form if kept outside in very hot weather?

  d This group is called the alkali metals. What are the names of groups II, VII and 0?

How did I do?

	✔
I can explain what is meant by an element.	☐
I can identify where metals and non-metals lie in the periodic table.	☐
I can recognise the symbols of the common elements.	☐
I can state the physical properties of the common elements.	☐

10: Molecules and compounds

Get started

When atoms bond together you get a molecule. Chemicals made from different types of atoms bonded together are called compounds. You can make compounds from elements using chemical reactions.

Practice

1. Explain why we call oxygen an element even though oxygen gas in the atmosphere is made from molecules.

2. Draw and label a diagram of a molecule of water.

3. In terms of the molecules, what is the difference between carbon monoxide and carbon dioxide?

4. When iron rusts, its mass increases. Where does this mass come from?

Challenge

5. a Explain the safety precautions you need to take when you burn magnesium in pure oxygen.

   b What compound is being formed?

   c Write down the word equation for this reaction.

   d Magnesium oxide does not consist of separate molecules. Explain how this can be so.

6. If you have 32 g of sulfur, you will always need 56 g of iron to react with it. If you supply 58 g of iron powder, 2 g of iron will remain once all of the sulfur has reacted.

   a Write down a word equation for the reaction between iron and sulfur.

   b One atom of iron combines with one atom of sulfur to produce the compound. Write down the symbol equation for the reaction.

   c Explain why the proportion of iron and sulfur reacting will always be the same.

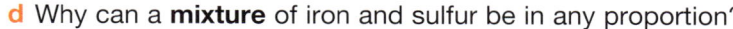

d Why can a **mixture** of iron and sulfur be in any proportion?

e How many times heavier is an iron atom compared to a sulfur atom?

7 This diagram shows the apparatus used for the reaction between sodium and chlorine.

a Explain why the chlorine doesn't escape up the tube.

b The reaction is started by applying a very small drop of water. Explain how this works.

c Sodium reacts very violently with chlorine. How could you tell this by looking at the flask?

d What is the purpose of the sand?

e Write down the word equation for this reaction.

f What is the common name for the compound produced?

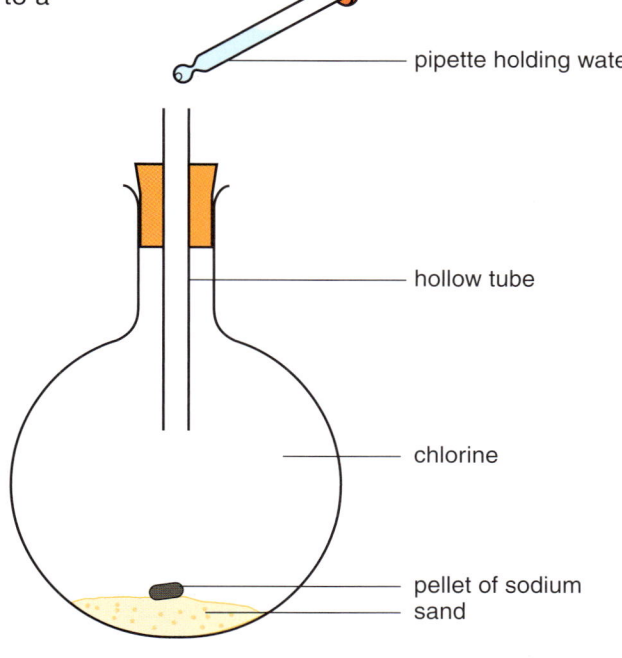

pipette holding water

hollow tube

chlorine

pellet of sodium
sand

8 Here is some apparatus for collecting chlorine from sea water.

a The gas from one of the electrodes is chlorine. Where does the chlorine originally come from?

b The gas from the other electrode gave a squeaky pop when a lighted splint was applied. What type of gas is this?

c Where did the gas discussed in part **b** originally come from?

d A solution of sodium hydroxide remains in the water. Write a word equation for the whole reaction.

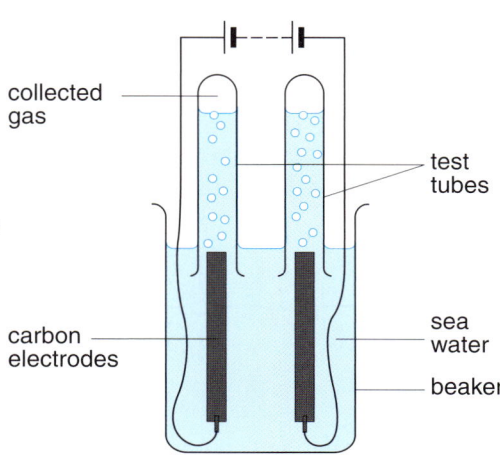

collected gas

test tubes

carbon electrodes

sea water

beaker

9 **a** Why do you often need heat to react two elements together?

b Explain why heat is often no longer needed once the reaction has started.

11: Chemical formulae

You will revise:

- how symbols and numbers can be used to describe a compound
- the meaning of symbol equations
- balancing symbol equations.

Get started

Elements and compounds can be represented by chemical formulae. These consist of the symbols of the elements involved. There are also numbers indicating the number of each atom in a molecule or the proportion of the elements in a compound.

Practice

1. What are the chemical formulae for water and hydrogen sulfide?

2. The formula for ammonia is NH_3. Describe the structure of an ammonia molecule.

3. State the formulae for sulfur dioxide and hydrochloric acid.

4. The formula for ammonium sulfate is $(NH_4)_2SO_4$. Assuming you have the minimum possible number of atoms, how many atoms of each element are present?

Challenge

5. The symbol for silicon dioxide is SiO_2. It does not form molecules but the atoms are joined together in a giant structure. What does the '2' mean in this context?

6. a Here is a diagram of a molecule of propane. Write down the chemical formula for this compound.

```
        H      H      H
        |      |      |
  H ─── C ─── C ─── C ─── H       Key:  H = Hydrogen atom
        |      |      |
        H      H      H                 C = Carbon atom
```

   b Pentane has five carbon atoms in a chain (with the corresponding hydrogen atoms added as in part a). What would the chemical formula be for pentane?

7. When you write symbol equations to represent chemical reactions, you have to be sure that the reactions are balanced by writing numbers in front of the terms. This means that the same number of atoms has to be represented on both sides of the equation.

   Here is an example: $2Mg + O_2 \rightarrow 2MgO$

Balance these equations.

a $CO_2 + C \rightarrow CO$

b $TiCl_4 + Na \rightarrow Ti + NaCl$

c $Ca(OH)_2 + HCl \rightarrow CaCl_2 + H_2O$

d $H_2 + O_2 \rightarrow H_2O$

e $Fe_2O_3 + Al \rightarrow Fe + Al_2O_3$

f $ZnS + O_2 \rightarrow ZnO + SO_2$

g $Fe_2O_3 + CO \rightarrow Fe + CO_2$

8 Sometimes the formula reflects the structure of a particular molecule. Here are two examples.

$$C_2H_5OH$$

$$CH_3CH(OH)CH_2OH$$

Write down the formulae of these molecules.

a

b

c

9 Balance this equation: $C_2H_6 + O_2 \rightarrow CO + H_2O$.

10 Look at the diagrams in question **8**. How many bonds do carbon atoms tend to form? What about the oxygen, nitrogen and hydrogen atoms? What is the difference between these atoms that makes them form a different number of bonds?

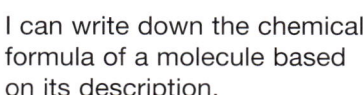

How did I do?

I can describe the structure of a molecule from its chemical formula. ☐

I can write down the chemical formula of a molecule based on its description. ☐

I can balance simple symbol equations. ☐

12: Mixtures

You will revise:

▶ the difference between a compound and a mixture

▶ how to separate mixtures by fractional distillation

▶ how mixtures affect cooling curves.

Get started

Mixtures of elements and compounds are not chemically combined and can be separated by physical means. Compounds and mixtures also behave differently when they are changing state.

Practice

1 Is a solution a compound or a mixture?

2 Explain why the elements in a compound are always in fixed proportions but the proportions in a mixture can vary.

3 What is meant by the decomposition of a compound? Write the word equation for the decomposition of silver chloride when light shines on it.

4 By measuring the temperature at which water boils (at standard atmospheric pressure), how can you tell if the water is impure?

Challenge

5 a Is air a compound or a mixture?

b Why do you find a lot of hydrogen at the top of the atmosphere but no hydrogen at the bottom?

c What are the two most abundant gases in the atmosphere at ground level?

d State the other gases that are also present.

e How can you use the different boiling points of the gases to separate them out?

6 a Where are the noble gases in the periodic table?

b Explain how William Ramsay discovered the noble gases neon, krypton and xenon in air.

c Having discovered argon four years earlier, Ramsay knew that these other noble gases must exist. Explain why this was the case.

7 Obtaining the individual gases from the air is an expensive process. Choose two of the gases present and explain why they are useful.

8 Here is a graph showing the cooling curve for a mixture of tin and lead.

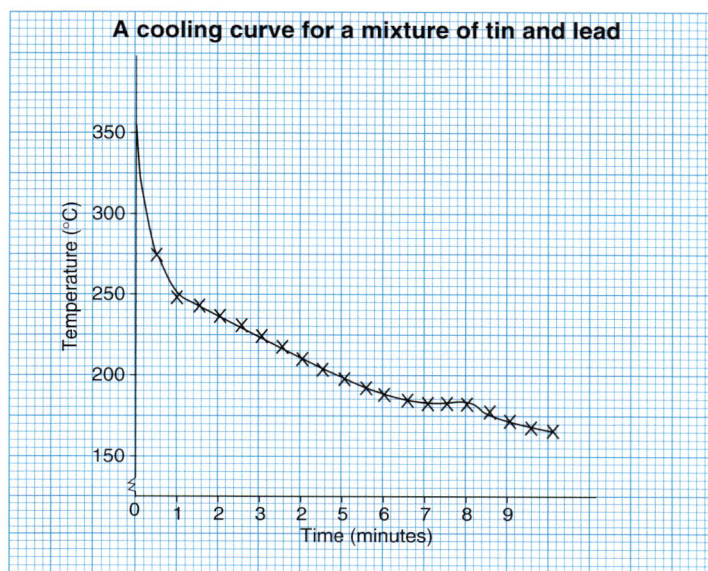

A cooling curve for a mixture of tin and lead

a Why couldn't you carry out this experiment in a school laboratory?

b The lead starts to freeze before the tin. At what temperature does this happen?

c What happens to the concentration of the tin in the liquid mixture after the lead begins to freeze?

d At what temperature does the whole mixture completely freeze?

e The melting point of lead is 327 °C and the melting point of tin is 232 °C. What do you notice about your answer to part d?

f A tin/lead mix has been used by plumbers for soldering pipes together. Explain why a wide-ranging melting point is useful in this instance.

9 Amalgams, alloys, gels and aerosols are all different types of mixtures. Find out what particular mixtures these terms refer to.

10 In terms of the particles involved, suggest why a mixture of tin and lead freezes at a lower temperature than the freezing temperature of either of the two substances.

How did I do?

I can explain why it is easier to separate mixtures than compounds. ☐

I can write about the gases found in air and how they are separated. ☐

I can discuss the main features of the cooling curve for a tin/lead mix. ☐

I can state other examples of mixtures such as aerosols and gels. ☐

13: Weathering of rocks

You will revise:

▸ the relationship between rocks and minerals

▸ an experiment to calculate the porosity of rocks

▸ different types of physical, chemical and biological weathering.

Get started

Over time rocks are gradually broken into smaller pieces by the effect of weathering. This process is an important part of the rock cycle. It also means that minerals end up in the soil.

Practice

1. Explain the difference between rocks and minerals.

2. State which of these materials are made from rock: fossils, grains of sand, clay, peat and diamond.

3. What is the difference between weathering and erosion?

4. Explain what is meant by physical and chemical weathering,

Challenge

5. a Unusually, what happens to the volume of water when it freezes?

   b Explain how this can lead to weathering of porous rocks.

   c What climate causes this type of weathering to happen the quickest?

6. A pupil did an experiment to find the porosity of some chalk. He placed a piece of chalk into 60 cm^3 of water in a measuring cylinder. The volume of the water rose to 85 cm^3. After 3 days the water level had decreased to 82 cm^3.

   a What is the volume of the chalk?

   b How much water did the chalk absorb? What have you assumed?

   c The porosity is calculated by dividing the volume of water absorbed by the volume of the rock and then multiplying by 100. Calculate the porosity of the chalk.

   The pupil repeated the experiment with a sample of granite. He found the porosity to be 1%.

   d Which sample, the chalk or the granite, will weather the quickest if the weathering is due to the expansion of water?

e Explain how the different structures of chalk and granite lead to such different porosities.

f Which of these rocks would be more useful at the bed of a reservoir?

7 a In the desert, there is a large difference in temperature between the day and the night. Explain how this might lead to the weathering of desert rocks.

b Why might a stone building in the middle of a forest need restoration earlier than a similar building that isn't in a forest? What is this type of weathering called?

8 This question is about the chemical weathering of rocks.

a What natural phenomenon leads to water dissolving carbon dioxide?

b The acid formed from water and carbon dioxide is called carbonic acid (H_2CO_3). Write a symbol equation for this reaction.

Carbonic acid reacts with limestone to form calcium hydrogen carbonate. Here is the reaction:

$$H_2CO_3 + CaCO_3 \rightarrow Ca(HCO_3)_2$$

c Write the name of the compound that limestone is made from.

d Calcium hydrogen carbonate is soluble in water. Explain how this leads to the erosion of limestone.

e Pollution from burning fossil fuels can increase levels of sulfur dioxide in the atmosphere. Explain how this can accelerate the rate of weathering.

9 The chemical reaction between carbonic acid and limestone in question **8** is reversible. Explain how this reaction can first lead to cave formations and then to stalactites and stalagmites.

10 By referring to the method of weathering in question **9**, explain why rocks get weaker and weaker with every cycle of freezing and thawing. What happens to the size of the cracks and the number of cracks? Why doesn't the rock break apart immediately?

11 Explain why rocks that have recently emerged from the Earth's crust already have cracks in them, even when no weathering has taken place.

How did I do?

	✔
I can explain the difference between rocks and minerals.	☐
I can explain measure the porosity of rocks.	☐
I can explain how the expansion of water can weather rocks.	☐
I can summarise the physical, chemical and biological processes of weathering.	☐

14: Sedimentary layers

You will revise:

▶ the transportation of sediment from rocks to the sea

▶ how sedimentary rocks are formed

▶ why fossils are found in sedimentary rocks.

Get started

Once rock has been fragmented by weathering it can be transported by various methods. Eventually the rock fragments (together with other materials) end up as sediment on the ocean floor. Over time these sedimentary layers can build up and form hard sedimentary rocks.

Practice

1 What is sediment?

2 Why do you get layers of sedimentary rocks?

3 Explain why most of the sediment eventually ends up on the ocean floor.

Challenge

4 This question is about the transportation of rock by rivers.

a Why do rivers tend to flow faster when they are near their source compared to when they are near the sea?

b Explain why rivers near their source can carry much bigger fragments of rock.

c What happens to the fragments of rock that are too big to be carried by the current?

d When you observe a river near its source you quite often see large boulders in the bed of the river. Under what conditions will these boulders move?

e Explain why fragments of rock on a river bed gradually get smaller with time.

f Why do the fragments of rock on a river bed get smaller the closer you get to the sea?

5 When a river goes round a bend, the side of the river on the outside of the bend flows faster than the side of the river on the inside of the bend.

a Explain why you often see a build up of sediment on the inside of the bend.

b Which side of the river will erode its bank the quickest?

c What happens to the position of the river banks over time?

6 **a** During the Ice Age, the transportation of sediment to the sea was at a much greater rate. What was the cause of this? Explain your answer.

b State one method of transporting sediment that is happening today that doesn't involve rivers.

7 Sedimentary rock often contains fossils. Explain why layers of exposed sedimentary rock contain older fossils lower down and younger fossils higher up.

8 Salt that was originally in sea water can be found in salt mines underground.

a Explain why you wouldn't find salt as a sediment at the bottom of the ocean.

b Describe a possible sequence of events that could produce a sediment of salt (think how you would achieve this in a lab).

c The rocks surrounding the layers of salt in a salt mine must be very dry. Explain why this is the case.

9 Calcium, like salt, also dissolves in sea water.

a Explain how the action of living sea creatures produces a sediment containing calcium at the bottom of the ocean.

b What sort of sedimentary rock does this calcium deposit become?

10 How did the discovery of fossil layers add weight to the evidence for the theory of evolution?

11 The sedimentary rock laid down at the time the dinosaurs became extinct contains the element iridium. Why was this an exciting find?

12 Describe how the fossil fuels were formed. How do oil companies locate potential drilling sites?

How did I do?

✔

I can describe why the sediment changes between the rocks and the sea. ☐

I can explain why the position of rivers changes over time. ☐

I can summarise how sedimentary rock can be formed at the bottom of the sea and in evaporating lakes. ☐

15: Types of rock

You will revise:
- the three main types of rock
- how each type is formed
- the main differences between them.

Get started

There are three main types of rock: igneous, sedimentary and metamorphic. They are all formed in different ways.

Practice

1 Which types of rock contain fossils?

2 Metamorphic rocks can be formed from which types of rock?

3 Under what conditions are metamorphic rocks produced?

4 Why are metamorphic rocks generally much harder than sedimentary rocks?

Challenge

5 **a** What type of rock is sandstone?

b You can begin the process of turning sand into sandstone by squeezing together wet sand. State what happens to the grains of sand in this process.

c In sandstone, minerals (such as calcium carbonate) act as a matrix holding the sand particles together. Describe how this matrix is formed.

d A geode is a hollow rock containing large crystals that have grown inside it. Explain how these crystals have been produced.

6 Here is a diagram of layers of sedimentary rock found in a valley in Namibia.

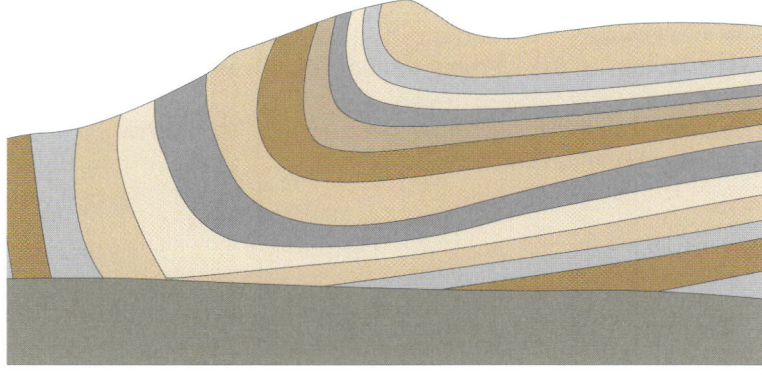

a Suggest what might have happened to produce this formation.

b Why is it likely that you will find some metamorphic rocks in this area?

c Explain why the same sedimentary rock turns into different types of metamorphic rock at different temperatures and pressures.

7 **a** In terms of their chemical composition, state one feature that all types of limestone have in common.

b In what way are different types of limestone different?

8 **a** Which type of metamorphic rock does limestone turn into?

Shale turns into slate at high temperatures and pressures.

b State two properties of slate that makes it useful for building roofs.

c State two features about the grains in shale that change when slate is formed.

d Why are the fossils found in slate often distorted?

e At higher temperatures and pressures, slate changes into phyllite, schist and finally gneiss. These rocks contain different minerals to the ones originally in the slate. Explain how these different minerals were formed.

9 **a** How is igneous rock formed?

b What is meant by intrusive and extrusive igneous rock?

10 For each rock listed, state whether it is sedimentary, metamorphic or igneous.

a Basalt   **b** Marble   **c** Granite

d Limestone   **e** Shale   **f** Slate

g Pumice   **h** Schist   **i** Gabbro

11 A very rare type of rock found on Earth's surface hasn't been formed by any of the processes you have investigated. What type of rock is this?

12 Why do over 90% of rocks contain silicates?

13 Explain why in some places metamorphic rocks only occur in small areas but in other places you get vast regions of metamorphic rocks.

How did I do?

	✔
I can write down the three main types of rock and how they were formed.	☐
I can explain why metamorphic rock is much denser than sedimentary rock.	☐
I can suggest likely places to find igneous and metamorphic rocks.	☐

16: The rock cycle

You will revise:
- extrusive and intrusive igneous rocks
- the role of temperature in the formation of igneous rocks
- the movement of material around the rock cycle.

Get started

Over millions of years, the materials that make up the rocks go round in a big cycle. Imagine what sort of journey a calcium atom might have made before it ends up in your bones.

Practice

1. How do the materials in igneous rocks end up in sedimentary rocks?

2. What do we call underground molten rock?

3. State two conditions that are needed to change metamorphic rocks into igneous rocks.

4. Why don't rocks have fixed melting points?

Challenge

5. a Use the particle model of matter to explain why crystals form when magma cools.

   b What type of rock is produced in this process?

   c Explain why the sizes of the crystals indicate the conditions under which the rock was made.

   d Manufacturers want to grow very large silicon crystals which they can then cut up to make silicon chips for computers. Suggest how they might grow these crystals.

6. Here is a diagram of a volcano.

   a Why are there layers of igneous rock?

   b Where would you find metamorphic rock in this diagram?

7. a Explain why extrusive igneous rocks are likely to have much smaller crystals than intrusive rocks.

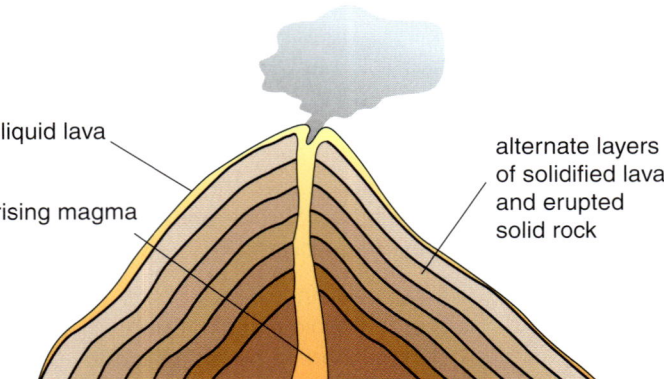

liquid lava

rising magma

alternate layers of solidified lava and erupted solid rock

vent

b Why can pumice float on water?

c Suggest one piece of evidence that pumice is an extrusive igneous rock.

8 Here is a table showing some data about different igneous rocks.

Type of rock	Intrusive or extrusive	Density (g/cm³)
Granite	Intrusive	2.7
Gabbro	Intrusive	3.0
Rhyolite	Extrusive	2.7
Basalt	Extrusive	3.0

a State which rock has the same chemical composition as gabbro.

b Identify two of these rocks that are relatively silica rich and two that are relatively iron rich.

c Suggest which type of rock is found in continental crust and which is found in oceanic crust (which lies lower down in the mantle).

9 Copy and complete this schematic diagram of the rock cycle.

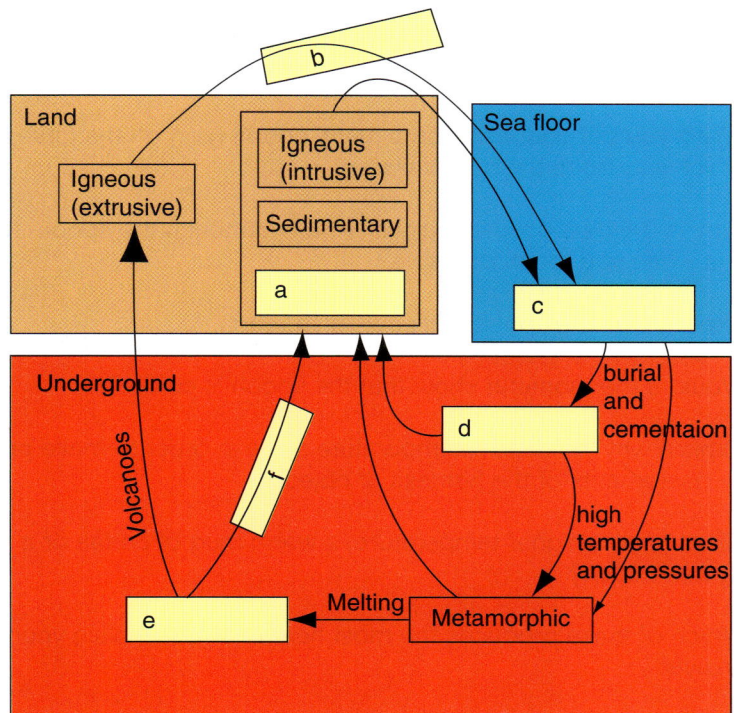

17: Heat and temperature

Get started

Although we can describe things we feel as hot or cold, we need to use a temperature scale to make proper scientific measurements. Transferring heat energy can make objects hotter or colder and it can also make them change their state.

Practice

1 Which quantity, heat or temperature, is a measure of the hotness of an object?

2 Describe an experiment where your left hand feels a bowl of water as hot, while your right hand feels the same water as cold.

3 In a solid, why do the particles vibrate on the spot?

4 What is the unit of heat energy?

Challenge

5 a Which is hotter, your hand or a wooden table (at room temperature)?

b When you put your hand on the table, which way does the heat energy transfer?

c When you put your hand on a metal spoon lying on the table, which way does the heat transfer?

d Why is the heat transfer quicker when you touch the spoon, than it is when you touch the table?

e Explain why the spoon feels colder to touch.

f Would a thermometer show that the spoon is colder?

g Explain why we need a temperature scale in order to make proper measurements of the hotness of objects.

6 a Which is at a higher temperature, a warm mug of coffee or a lighted match?

b Which of these produces the most heat energy? Explain your answer.

7 You have a bowl of crushed ice in water.

a What temperature would this bowl be (at normal atmospheric pressure)?

b At first, what would happen to the crushed ice and water if you transferred heat energy away from the bowl (by placing it in a freezer)?

c How could you tell if the temperature falls below the value you stated in part **a** simply by looking at the bowl?

d If, instead, you were transferring heat energy to the bowl, how could you tell when the temperature goes above this value?

e What similar situation occurs at 100 °C?

f Describe how you could add a scale to an alcohol thermometer to measure the temperature in centigrade.

8 **a** What is the main difference, in terms of the particles, between a solid when it is cold and when it is hot?

Here is a graph of the temperature of some paraffin wax when it is heated using a Bunsen burner. Paraffin wax is a solid at room temperature.

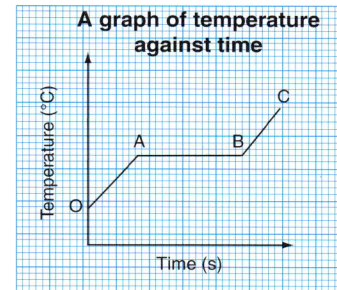

A graph of temperature against time

b What is happening to the particles:

i in the region OA,

ii in the region AB,

iii in the region BC?

c Why doesn't the temperature increase in the region AB?

d What would the graph look like if you continued to heat the paraffin?

9 When liquids freeze to become solids, they give heat energy out without reducing their temperature. Where does this heat energy come from?

10 If you plot the temperature of a hot mug of coffee against time, you get a cooling curve. Why does the graph curve?

11 What is a Galileo thermometer? How does it work?

How did I do?

I can work out the direction that heat energy is transferred between objects of different temperatures. ☐

I can explain why metals feel colder than non-metals when they are at the same temperature. ☐

I can state what happens to the temperature and the heat energy when objects are changing state. ☐

18: Heat transfer

You will revise:
- the three main methods of heat transfer
- how to explain conduction and convection in terms of particles
- how we can reduce heat transfer using insulating materials.

Get started

Heat is transferred from hotter objects to colder objects. The rate at which the heat is transferred depends on the temperature difference and on the 'ease' with which the transfer takes place. There are three main methods of heat transfer: conduction, convection and radiation.

Practice

1. Explain what is meant by insulation.

2. A string vest contains lots of holes. How do the holes keep the wearer warm?

3. Explain how a vacuum flask can keep hot things hot and cold things cold.

4. Why can you only get convection in liquids and gases?

Challenge

5. You have a steel rod. One end of the rod is hot and the other end is cold.

   a What form of energy is affected by how fast objects are moving?

   b Describe how this type of energy varies along the rod.

   c After a while, heat has conducted along the rod so that the rod is all at the same temperature. Rewrite your answer to part **b** for this new situation.

   d Explain how the heat energy has been transferred along the rod.

6. Here is a diagram of some water and ice being heated in a test tube.

   a Explain the purpose of the gauze.

   b The top of the water is boiling, while the bottom of the tube is still cold. What does this tell you about the water?

   c Why wouldn't this experiment work in a copper container?

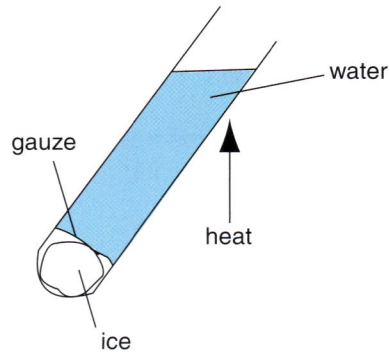

7 In general, why are solids better conductors than liquids and liquids better conductors than gases?

8 **a** Explain, in terms of particles, why materials expand when they are heated.

b Once a fluid has expanded, what happens to its density and why does it rise?

9 This diagram shows some smoke being drawn through a glass chimney.

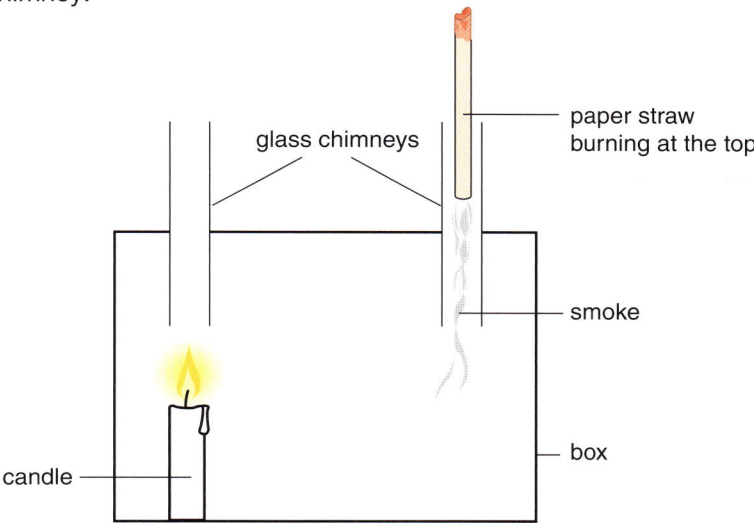

a Explain why the smoke moves down through the chimney.

b If the straw was placed above the other chimney, what would happen?

c What do we call this method of heat transfer?

10 An essential source of energy on the Earth is heat energy from the Sun. Explain why there must be another method of heat transfer other than conduction and convection.

11 Why are metals such good conductors of heat?

12 How do most methods of house insulation work?

13 Why do metal teapots keep tea hot for longer if their surfaces are shiny?

14 If fridges extract heat energy from the food, where does this heat energy go?

How did I do?

	✔
I can describe conduction and convection in terms of particles.	☐
I understand why heat from the Sun can be transferred by radiation only.	☐
I can explain ways of reducing the amount of conduction, convection and radiation from hot objects.	☐

19: Magnetism

You will revise:
- magnets and magnetic materials
- the domain theory of magnetism
- magnetic fields produced by current-carrying wires and solenoids.

Get started

Magnets, magnetic materials and wires carrying electric currents feel forces acting on them when they are inside a magnetic field. The nature of this force can be explored by using ideas about magnetic poles, field lines and domains.

Practice

1. Which of these materials are magnetic and which are non-magnetic: tin, cobalt, mercury, nickel, iron oxide, iron sulfide?

2. Write down the combinations of poles that attract and the combinations of poles that repel.

3. Why is one end of a bar magnet called a N pole?

4. What is the difference between a magnet and a magnetic material?

5. What is magnetic shielding? How would you magnetically shield a spaceship?

Challenge

6. A pupil investigated some metal bars (A to F) that looked exactly the same. Her teacher asked her to identify whether the bars were magnetic, made out of magnetic material (but not magnetised) or not made of a magnetic material at all. From her results below, identify the category of each bar.

   Bar A attracted some iron filings (the filings weren't magnetised).

   Bar A attracted bar B.

   Bar A repelled bar C.

   Bar D turned and pointed due north when it was suspended in the air.

   Bar B didn't pick up any iron filings.

   Bar E didn't point due north when suspended in the air but a small compass did point towards it.

   Bar F wasn't attracted by bar D and it didn't pick up any iron filings.

7 One model of magnetic materials describes them as having lots of tiny magnets (called domains) inside. Each tiny magnet can be represented by an arrow, with the arrow head representing the N pole.

  a Here are some diagrams representing three magnetic materials. Which one is unmagnetised, which is slightly magnetised and which is completely magnetised?

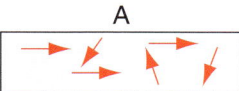
A

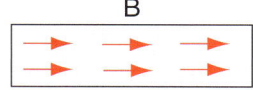
B

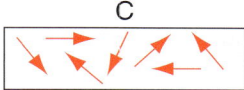
C

  b Why is there a limit to how strongly you can magnetise some iron?

  c Why does heating a magnet make it lose its magnetism?

8 **a** What is a magnetic field?

  b Which direction do field lines point: towards the N pole of the magnet or towards the S pole?

  c How can you tell, by looking at the field lines, where the magnetic field is the strongest?

  d How does the strength of a magnetic field change as the distance increases?

  e If Earth's magnetic field was produced by a bar magnet, which pole of the magnet would be pointing due north?

  f Sketch the shape of the magnetic field produced by the Earth.

9 Here are two magnetic fields produced by current-carrying wires. What is the arrangement of the wires that have produced them?

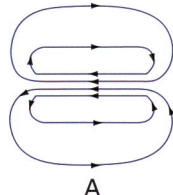
A

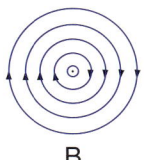
B

10 One way of magnetising a magnetic material is to point the material due north and hammer it very gently. How does this work?

11 A current-carrying solenoid produces a weak magnetic field. Why does placing an iron nail inside the solenoid make the magnetic field much stronger?

How did I do?

I can explain how a magnet behaves differently from a magnetic material. ☐

I can describe the domain theory of magnetism. ☐

I can recognise the magnetic fields produced from single current-carrying wires and solenoids. ☐

20: Using magnetism

You will revise:
- electromagnets
- buzzers and bells
- relays and circuit breakers.

Get started

An electromagnet enables you to turn magnetic forces on and off at the flick of a switch. This has resulted in many useful devices.

Practice

1. What are the basic components of an electromagnet?

2. State two things you can do to make an electromagnet stronger.

3. How could you change the S pole of an electromagnet into a N pole without moving it?

4. What happens to the electromagnet when you turn the current off?

Challenge

5.
   a What is the difference between an a.c. and a d.c. current?

   b What is happening to an a.c. current for the split second that it is at 0 A?

   c Describe how you can use this effect to make a buzzer using an electromagnet and a springy steel blade.

   d Explain why an electromagnet connected to an a.c. supply can still pick up a steel paper clip.

6.
   a What is a relay? What is it used for?

   b The diagram shows part of a relay. Explain how it works.

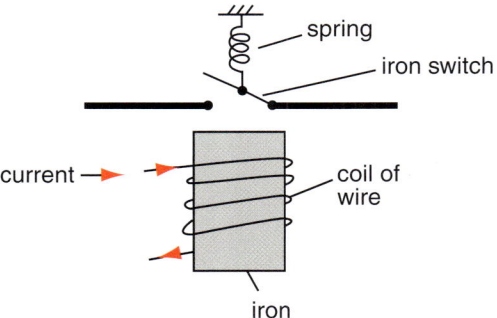

7 A pupil adapts the relay shown in question **6** to make a model of a circuit breaker. He turns the switch upside down and places the spring above the switch. This means that the spring keeps the switch closed when the electromagnet is off but when the current is supplied to the electromagnet, it tries to pull the switch open against the pull of the spring.

   a Circuit breakers are safety devices that break the circuit if the current gets too large. Explain how this one might work.

   b What would happen if the current supplied to the electromagnet did stop flowing? Why would this be a potential problem for this design of circuit breaker?

8 Here is a diagram of an electric bell.

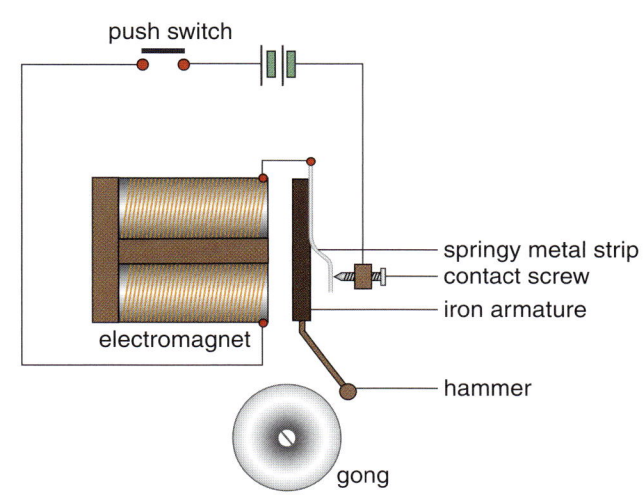

push switch

springy metal strip
contact screw
iron armature

electromagnet

hammer

gong

   a When the switch is closed, what happens to the electromagnet?

   b How does this result in the hammer striking the gong?

   c Why does the electromagnet switch off at this stage?

   d What happens to the hammer once the electromagnet has switched off?

   e Why does the electromagnet switch back on again?

   f Explain how the hammer continues to repetitively strike the gong.

9 What is the difference between a soft and a hard magnetic material? So why is iron used in electromagnets rather than steel?

10 Why does the melting temperature of copper wire limit the strength of electromagnets? How can superconductors solve this problem?

11 By mistake a pupil winding the wire round an iron nail starts winding in the opposite direction halfway along the nail. In terms of the domains in the iron explain why the electromagnet won't work.

How did I do?

I can suggest and explain two things you can do to make an electromagnet stronger. ☐

Given a diagram of an electric bell, I can explain how it works. ☐

I can describe how a relay and a circuit breaker work. ☐

21: Light and reflection

You will revise:
- the nature of light and how it travels
- angles of incidence and reflection
- images in mirrors.

Get started

Light is a special kind of electromagnetic wave that we can detect when it enters our eyes. It moves very quickly in straight lines and it interacts with different materials in different ways.

Practice

1. What is the special name that we give to the speed that light travels in a vacuum?

2. Explain the difference between a transparent and a translucent material.

3. What type of materials form shadows?

4. Where do we see the image in a mirror: in front of it, on its surface, or behind it?

Challenge

5. A teacher sets up a demonstration of a laser beam.

   a What safety precautions should you take when using a laser?

   b Explain why pupils could only see the patch of light where the laser beam hit the wall rather than the beam itself.

   c The teacher then sprayed some deodorant into the room. Explain why pupils could now observe the beam.

   d What shape of path did the beam follow?

6. Light can be both transmitted and reflected at the surface of a piece of glass such as a shop window.

   a If both transmission and reflection take place, what do you see when you look through the window into the shop?

   b Why does the inside of the shop look a lot clearer when you are looking through the window at night time (assuming the shop lights are on)?

   c The shopkeeper fitted windows that didn't absorb as much light. How did the view looking into the shop change?

7 This diagram shows how a ray of light from a raybox is reflected by a mirror.

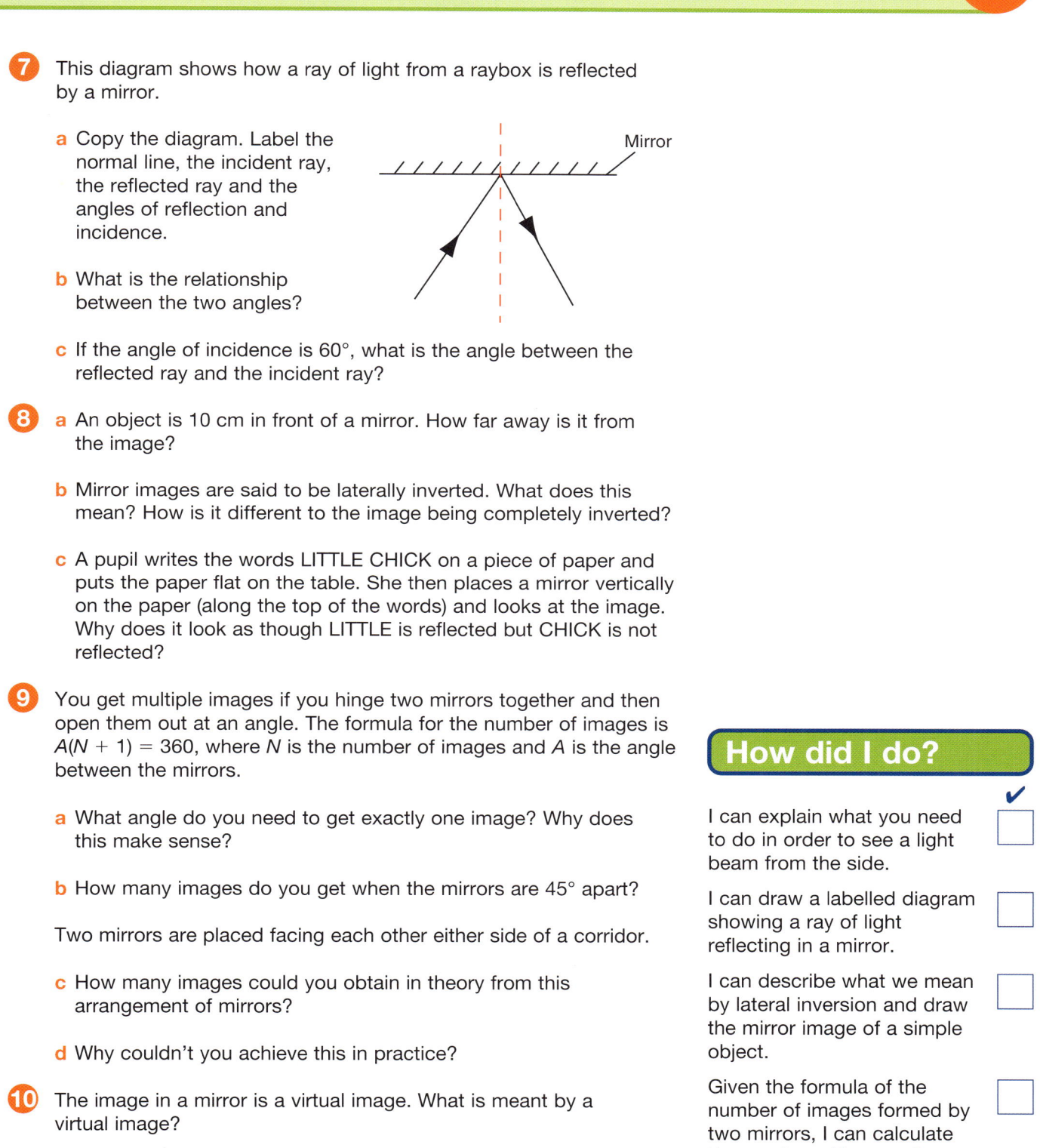

a Copy the diagram. Label the normal line, the incident ray, the reflected ray and the angles of reflection and incidence.

Mirror

b What is the relationship between the two angles?

c If the angle of incidence is 60°, what is the angle between the reflected ray and the incident ray?

8 a An object is 10 cm in front of a mirror. How far away is it from the image?

b Mirror images are said to be laterally inverted. What does this mean? How is it different to the image being completely inverted?

c A pupil writes the words LITTLE CHICK on a piece of paper and puts the paper flat on the table. She then places a mirror vertically on the paper (along the top of the words) and looks at the image. Why does it look as though LITTLE is reflected but CHICK is not reflected?

9 You get multiple images if you hinge two mirrors together and then open them out at an angle. The formula for the number of images is $A(N + 1) = 360$, where N is the number of images and A is the angle between the mirrors.

a What angle do you need to get exactly one image? Why does this make sense?

b How many images do you get when the mirrors are 45° apart?

Two mirrors are placed facing each other either side of a corridor.

c How many images could you obtain in theory from this arrangement of mirrors?

d Why couldn't you achieve this in practice?

10 The image in a mirror is a virtual image. What is meant by a virtual image?

11 What is the speed of light in a vacuum? How do we use this to define a light-year?

22: Refraction and colour

You will revise:
▶ refraction
▶ separating white light into the visible spectrum
▶ colour mixing.

Get started

Light rays can change speed when they pass from one medium to another. This makes them change direction if they pass through the interface at an angle. Different colours of light bend by different amounts, which means that white light splits into the visible spectrum when it passes through a triangular prism.

Practice

1 What is meant by refraction?

2 State the name given to the phenomenon of splitting light up into its constituent colours.

3 Explain the difference between primary and secondary colours.

4 When you shine white light onto a pair of blue jeans, why do they look blue?

Challenge

5 The diagram below shows a ray of light entering a glass block.

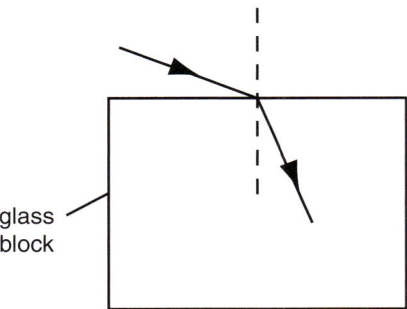

glass block

a Copy the diagram and label the incident ray, the refracted ray, the normal line and the angles of refraction and incidence.

b What also happens to the light ray at the interface?

c Why does the light ray change direction?

d In general, what is different about the angle of refraction and the angle of incidence for rays entering a glass block?

e What is the special case where the angle of incidence equals the angle of refraction?

6 Explain why a swimming pool looks shallower than it actually is.

7 **a** Why does white light split into several colours when it passes through a triangular prism.

b What is the name given to the band of colours produced from this effect?

c How did Newton use a second prism to show that the green light from the visible spectrum was a pure colour?

8 A teacher shone overlapping circles of red, green and blue light onto a screen. The diagram shows what the screen looked like.

Copy the diagram and fill in the missing colours.

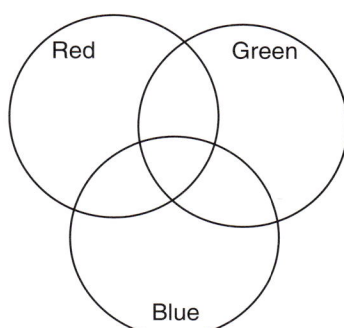

9 Explain why a magenta pair of trousers looks blue when they are in cyan-coloured light.

10 Copy and complete this table about the appearance of different coloured clothes in different coloured lights.

Colour of clothing (in white light)	Colour in red light	Colour in blue light	Colour in green light	Colour in yellow light	Colour in cyan light	Colour in magenta light
Red	Red	Black		Red	Black	
Blue						
Green						
Yellow						
Cyan						

11 What is the difference between compound yellow and pure yellow light?

12 What colour would a red shirt appear in pure yellow light?

13 Why do our eyes perceive pure yellow and compound yellow as the same colour?

How did I do?

	✔
I can draw a labelled diagram of a ray passing through a rectangular glass block.	☐
I can explain why white light splits into the visible spectrum in a prism.	☐
I can draw three overlapping circles and label the primary colours, the secondary colours and where we see white light.	☐
I can work out what colour objects look like in different coloured lights.	☐

23: Sound waves

You will revise:
- how sound is produced and how sound waves travel
- using an oscilloscope to represent a sound wave
- the effect of altering pitch and volume on the shape of a sound wave.

Get started

Vibrations can travel through the air or another medium as sound. The nature of these vibrations determines what sort of sound we hear.

Practice

1. Why can't sound waves pass through a vacuum?

2. How does the speed of sound vary in solids, liquids and gases?

3. What is the frequency of a sound wave? What unit is it measured in?

4. How does the amplitude of a wave vary if it is carrying more energy?

Challenge

5. a What do the strings of a guitar have to do in order to produce sound?

   b State two things you can do to make a guitar string produce a higher pitched note.

   c How else do the different guitar strings produce the different pitches?

6. This diagram shows traces of sound waves on an oscilloscope screen.

   A ∿∿∿∿   B ∿∿∿   C ∿∿∿∿   D ∿∿

   a Which trace has the highest frequency?

   b Which traces are from sounds at the same pitch?

   c Describe the sound that is producing trace D.

   d Which traces have the same amplitude?

   e How do the sounds producing traces B and C differ?

   f If the microphone connected to trace A is moved further away from the sound source, how would the trace change? Without altering the sound, how could you make the trace look the same again?

7 A sitar and a harp produce two notes at the same pitch and volume yet they sound very different.

   a State two similarities between the two sound waves they produce.

   b How would the oscilloscope traces differ?

8 A hydrophone is a device that can pick up sounds under water. Here is a diagram of a simple one that you can make.

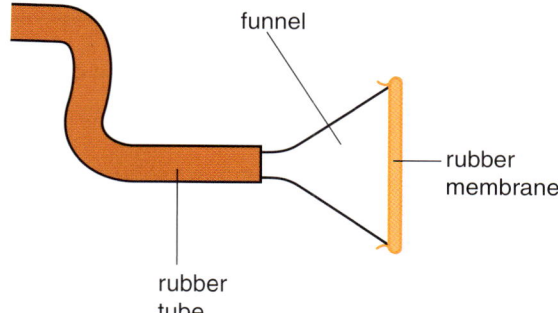

funnel

rubber membrane

rubber tube

   a Describe, in terms of the particles involved, how the sound from the water is carried through the hydrophone.

   b How does the funnel help to amplify the sound?

   c In which direction do the air particles vibrate in the rubber tube?

   d Explain why you can't hear an underwater animal when your ear is above the surface of the water but you can hear it quite clearly when your ear is under the water.

9 **a** Explain why the speed of sound in solids is faster than it is in liquids.

   b Why can you hear that a train is coming for a long time before it actually appears?

   c Why can whale song be heard over a much greater distance in water than in air?

   d Why does the sound produced by an earthquake arrive at exactly the same time as the actual earthquake?

10 When you cup your hands over your mouth, the person directly in front of you can hear you more clearly. Explain how this works.

11 Explain why a pitch at 3000 Hzs sounds louder than a pitch at 100 Hz even though the amplitude is the same. Why do babies cry at a pitch of 3000 Hz?

How did I do?

I can explain why sound travels differently in gases, liquids and solids.   ✔

I can state three ways in which you can change the pitch of the sound produced by a vibrating string.

I can relate pitch and volume to frequency and amplitude of a sound wave.

24: Hearing sound

You will revise:

▶ the structure of the human ear and how sound energy travels through it

▶ problems that people can have with their hearing

▶ artificial aids that can help with these problems.

Get started

The ear converts vibrations in the air into electrical signals that are passed to the brain. Unfortunately some people are born with hearing impairments, and hearing can be damaged by excessive noise and ageing. Artificial aids can sometimes help.

Practice

1 What is the normal frequency range of human hearing?

2 How does this range change as you get older?

3 What scale do we use to describe the loudness of noise?

Challenge

4 Here is a diagram of the human ear.

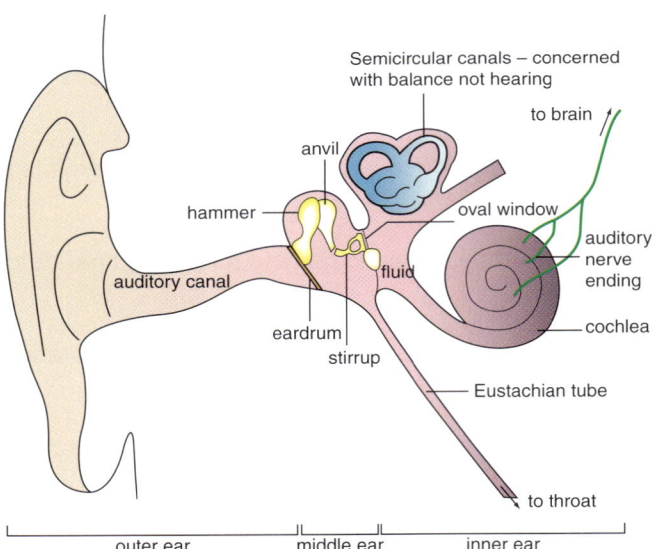

Semicircular canals – concerned with balance not hearing

to brain

anvil

hammer

oval window

auditory canal

fluid

auditory nerve ending

eardrum

cochlea

stirrup

Eustachian tube

to throat

outer ear | middle ear | inner ear

a Describe in as much detail as you can how the energy from the sound wave entering the ear ends up as an electrical signal in the auditory nerve.

b State two advantages of the outer ear being funnel shaped.

c The ossicles (hammer, anvil and stirrup) act like levers. This means that the stirrup moves much more then the hammer. Explain how this amplifies the sound.

d The ossicles also reduce the amount of reflection of the sound wave when it passes into the inner ear. Why would a lot of reflection be a problem?

e Explain the advantage of having fluid inside the ear.

f Suggest why the cochlea is spiral shaped.

5 a Some hearing devices turn sound waves into vibrations in the skull. Explain how this can help some people who have hearing impairments.

b There is a part of the ear that, if damaged, will result in a hearing impairment that can't be helped with today's technology. Which part is it?

c Most hearing aids amplify the sound electronically. Why is it important for an audiologist to test the patient's hearing at lots of different frequencies before they program a hearing aid?

6 The threshold of hearing is given a value of 0 on the decibel scale.

a What is meant by the threshold of hearing?

b If somebody has a threshold of 40 dB, can they hear sounds easily or is their hearing impaired? Explain your answer.

7 Here is a graph of how the threshold of hearing varies with frequency for a normal ear.

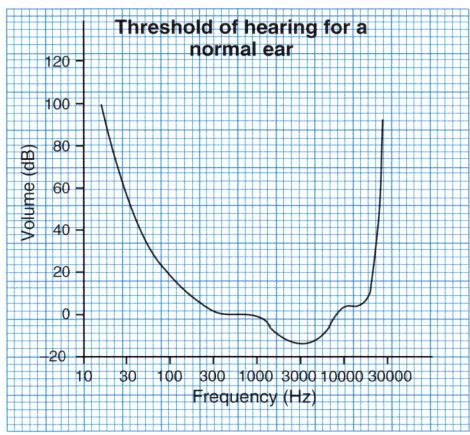

a Which frequency is the ear most sensitive to?

b Why is this important for designers of fire alarms?

c State two ways in which the graph would change for a much older person.

Answers

1 Food

1 Proteins, carbohydrates, fats, vitamins, minerals.
2 Proteins: growth and repair; carbohydrates: energy and fibres for preventing constipation; fats: energy and cell membranes; vitamins: many uses, including seeing, nerve function, digestion of calcium; minerals: many uses, including calcium for bones, iron for haemoglobin.
3 It is a diet in which the body gets the nutrients it needs in the right amounts.
4 People have different lifestyles and different metabolisms.
5 a 35 kg.
  b i Water is used in sweat. ii Water is a solvent and allows dissolved chemicals to move around the body with the plasma in the bloodstream.
  c Unlike water, the body stores reserves of food and can begin to digest them if things get really bad.
6 a Carbon and hydrogen.
  b The molecules have varying numbers of carbon, oxygen and hydrogen atoms within them.
  c Fibre: cereals; starch: potatoes; sugar: chocolates.
  d Fibre makes the digested food more solid, helping the muscles in the gut to push the food along.
  e They provide the body with energy.
7 a Proteins are long chains of amino acids.
  b Building structures such as muscles; forming enzymes to aid digestion.
  c For example, meats, dairy products, fish, pulses.
  d Meats and dairy products provide most of the protein in non-vegetarian diets.
8 a Add iodine solution.
  b Sugar.
  c Biuret test: add food to water, then add sodium hydroxide and copper sulfate solutions.
  d Fat.
9 a A is chicken, B is pasta.
  b They don't provide enough of the other nutrient groups.
  c Type A: pregnant woman or growing child who needs a lot of protein for growth; type B: athlete who needs a lot of carbohydrate for energy.
10 a Very pale and devoid of energy (iron).
  b Bandy legs in children and soft bones (vitamin D).
  c Nerves stop working properly leading to weak muscles (vitamin B1).
  d Bleeding of gums and under the skin (vitamin C).

2 Digestion

1 To break large insoluble molecules into smaller, soluble ones.
2 Food is physically broken up into smaller pieces. The amylase enzyme starts to break down carbohydrates. Mucin in the saliva coats the food to make it easier to swallow.
3 They are called enzymes and they are made from proteins.
4 The enzyme pepsin, which breaks down protein, needs acidic conditions to work properly.
5 a Biting into softer foods.
  b Ripping apart tougher foods.
  c Grinding foods.
6 a i Oesophagus; ii stomach; iii liver; iv gall bladder; v pancreas; vi small intestine; vii large intestine.
  b It is a collection of organs working together to perform a general task.
  c liver, gall bladder and pancreas.
  d They secrete digestive juices containing enzymes.
7 a It produces pepsin.
  b It produces hydrochloric acid.
  c Muscles contract in waves along the walls, allowing food to thoroughly mix with digestive juices.
  d It stops the stomach digesting itself.
8 a They neutralise the food from the stomach, allowing the other digesting enzymes to work.
  b It makes enzymes to aid digestion; it absorbs digested food through its walls.
  c They dramatically increase the surface area making digestion much more efficient.
9 a It absorbs water and dissolved vitamins from the food, forming faeces.
  b Bacteria and fibre.
  c So that the products of digestion can enter the bloodstream easily.
10 a Amylase.
  b Pepsin.
  c Stomach.
  d Fat.

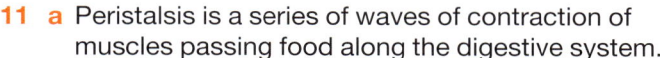

11 a Peristalsis is a series of waves of contraction of muscles passing food along the digestive system.
   b The movement of food doesn't rely on gravity.
12 The liver processes the digested food; for example, it converts excess sugars into glycogen.
13 Bile is alkaline, so it neutralises the environment in the small intestine. It emulsifies (breaks up into small globules of liquid) fats to provide a larger surface area for the enzymes to work on.
14 Glucose is absorbed by the small intestine wall and so must go through the capillaries into the veins. Then it goes from the veins to the heart to the lungs, back to the heart, then to cells via arteries and capillaries.

3 Respiration

1 Germinating peas are respiring and the chemical reaction produces heat. Place the peas in an enclosed flask with a thermometer; compare with a flask containing boiled (and obviously dead!) peas as a control.
2 Glucose + oxygen → carbon dioxide + water (+ energy).
3 They are both reactions with oxygen and both produce energy.
4 Respiration is a much slower reaction (at a lower temperature) and is controlled by catalysts.
5 $C_6H_{12}O_6 + 6O_2 \rightarrow 6CO_2 + 6H_2O$. It releases energy from glucose.
6 a Carbon dioxide.
   b The right-hand tube of limewater goes milky.
   c The left-hand tube stays clear. Since the air you breathe in bubbles through this tube, this must mean that it contains less carbon dioxide.
7 Water. Test for this by using anhydrous cobalt chloride paper to see if it turns from blue to pink.
8 a Nitrogen.
   b This depends on the humidity in the weather.
   c The water in exhaled air comes from the moist surfaces of the respiratory system so is fairly constant.
   d It comes (mainly) from the products of respiration.
9 a To stop photosynthesis which would remove the carbon dioxide from the solution.
   b Orange-red to yellow.
   c The levels of carbon dioxide are not high enough.
   d Plants get their glucose from the photosynthesis reaction.

10 a Mammals are warm blooded; they need a lot more energy to maintain their body temperatures.
   b Some plants and animals can respire and photosynthesise underwater.
11 The breakdown of glucose without oxygen.
12 Glucose breaks down to form carbon dioxide and alcohol. The alcohol is used in the beer; the carbon dioxide is used to make the bread rise. Alcohol evaporates out of the bread when you cook it.
13 It promotes the formation of haemoglobin (due to lack of oxygen) ready to transport the oxygen more efficiently when the athlete returns to lower altitude.

4 Blood circulation and breathing

1 Haemoglobin in the red blood cells transports oxygen; the plasma carries the others.
2 Breathing in.
3 It contracts and flattens to make the chest cavity larger. This makes air rush in. You then breathe out by relaxing the diaphragm.
4 Capillaries are tiny blood vessels whose walls are about one cell thick. They are useful because substances can easily pass through them to and from the bloodstream.
5 Breathing is used to provide oxygen and to remove carbon dioxide and water vapour. The bloodstream is used to transport oxygen (and glucose) to the cells and carbon dioxide and water to the lungs.
6 a They provide a huge surface area.
   b Water dissolves the gases, allowing easy passage to and from the blood.
   c Oxygen moves from the alveolar duct to the blood; carbon dioxide goes the other way.
   d The lungs need enough blood to keep up with the rate of gaseous exchange.
7 a A is an artery and B is a vein.
   b Veins contain valves but arteries don't.
   c Arteries carry blood away from the heart; veins deliver blood to the heart.
   d Most veins carry blood away from cells that have respired; most arteries carry blood to the cells and so contain oxygen.
8 Blood comes out of left ventricle and goes through the body; blood from the body enters the right atrium; blood from right ventricle goes through the lungs and then returns to the left atrium.

9 a Fact A.

   b Blood travels in one direction through the veins.

   c The side that swells up is where the blood is flowing from. Therefore blood flows through the veins towards the heart and through the arteries away from the heart.

   d The animals were alive since the heart must be beating to make the blood flow.

10 The cross-sectional area of capillaries is much smaller than that of the arteries.

11 Oxygen can easily attach and detach itself from haemoglobin. Therefore it can be actively transported and delivered to where it is needed.

12 The pulmonary vein carries oxygenated blood from the lungs to the heart.

13 The kidneys filter the blood, keeping the various chemicals in the blood at normal levels.

5 Micro-organisms

1 It is a very tiny organism that can't be seen by the unaided eye.

2 Bacteria can reproduce by themselves; viruses need the help of infected cells.

3 Fungi release spores which grow into new organisms if the conditions are favourable.

4 A parasite lives in another organism and uses it to provide a favourable environment and food.

5 a i Cell wall; **ii** cytoplasm; **iii** genetic material.

   b Bacteria don't have a nucleus.

   c They secrete digestive juices out of their cell walls and absorb the dissolved food back in.

6 a The instruments aren't carrying any micro-organisms.

   b Gamma radiation.

   c Heat them strongly.

   d To make sure that the micro-organisms you find are due to the experiment you are doing and weren't there anyway.

   e To make sure that your micro-organism colony doesn't cause any diseases.

7 a It provides the right nutrients.

   b Place them in an incubator at a warm temperature.

8 a Bacteria can be seen through an optical microscope. To see viruses you need an electron microscope.

   b Viruses need living cells to reproduce.

   c A protein coat and genetic material.

9 a 2 bacteria.

   b $2^{48} \approx 2.8 \times 10^{14}$ bacteria.

   c $(2.8 \times 10^{14})^3 \approx 2.2 \times 10^{43}$ (28 million million) bacteria.

   d There wouldn't be enough resources in the agar jelly to cope with this size of population.

10 a Independent: quantity of sugar; dependent: amount of carbon dioxide.

   b Amount of yeast; temperature.

   c Incubate the dough in a measuring cylinder and measure the volume of the dough before and after incubating.

   d Plot the volume of carbon dioxide on the y-axis and the quantity of sugar on the x-axis. You would expect a positive correlation since sugar is a reactant of respiration and carbon dioxide is a product.

   e The warmth speeds up the respiration of the yeast so more CO_2 is produced. This CO_2 produces bubbles in the dough to give the bread the right texture.

   f Fungus.

11 Bacteria don't reproduce as quickly at cold temperatures. Hence the rate of decomposition of the food and the release of toxins is slower.

12 It is where two organisms share the same environment to the benefit of both organisms. Natural bacteria in our digestive system can help us digest our food properly.

6 Fighting diseases

1 A pathogen.

2 Vectors are animals that carry pathogens from one diseased organism to another.

3 Bacteria.

4 They release harmful toxins.

5 a The skin.

   b It kills many bacteria by disrupting their cell walls.

   c The orifices (entrances) of the body and through open wounds.

   d Mucus traps micro-organisms in the mouth and nose.

   e These cells waft the mucus up to the mouth. The mucus is then swallowed, passing the bacteria into the digestive system where they are destroyed or excreted.

   f They form blood clots which quickly close up open wounds before the skin can repair itself.

6 a Phagocytes surround micro-organisms and destroy them; lymphocytes detect antigens on the micro-organisms and release antibodies that

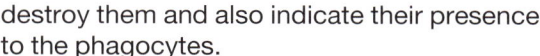

destroy them and also indicate their presence to the phagocytes.

b Micro-organisms have antigens on their surface which are specific to that particular organism.

c An antibody is a chemical that lymphocytes produce that is specific to a particular antigen. They latch onto antigens, start to kill the pathogen and attract the attention of the phagocytes.

d Antibodies remain in the blood once the pathogen has been dealt with ready to act quickly if the body becomes re-infected before any symptoms are apparent.

7 a Fleming noticed that the bacteria colony didn't grow near some mould that had accidentally landed on the agar jelly.

b There are regions around the antibiotic where no bacteria have survived.

c The one with the largest region where no bacteria have colonised.

d There is no antibiotic that will kill all types of bacteria.

e Bacteria can reproduce very quickly; you need to make sure that you have killed all of them before you finish the antibiotic or the colony will grow again and re-infect.

8 a Viruses can't be killed by conventional drugs.

b The babies have absorbed antibodies from their mother's blood in the womb and from breast milk after they have been born.

c Vaccinations deliberately infect a person with a less harmful version of the virus. The body produces antibodies to this virus which remain in the blood. If the more serious form of the virus infects the body, the antibodies can act to destroy the virus before it has any harmful effects.

9 The immune system gets confused and thinks that normal body cells are foreign. Hence the body attacks itself.

10 We are selectively breeding the types of bacteria that are resistant to antibiotics.

11 A huge number of different viruses produce colds. Just because we become immune to one type of cold virus doesn't mean that we are immune to all of them.

12 An epidemic is widespread infection throughout a region; a pandemic is an epidemic of worldwide proportions. A pandemic is more likely today due to increased air travel between countries.

7 Classifying animals and plants

1 Vertebrates have a backbone; invertebrates don't.

2 Mammals, birds, reptiles, amphibians, fish.

3 Plants can produce their own energy (through photosynthesis); animals can't do this and so need to eat food.

4 You can look at their obvious features first to narrow down the search and then look at the organism in greater detail. This works in the same way as finding a book in a library.

5 a Sac-like body and tentacles.
  b Flatworms.
  c Long flat bodies.
  d Long segmented bodies.
  e Arthropods.
  f Possess a rotation symmetry of order 5.
  g Molluscs.

6 a There are still many different species within each group with subgroups of similar characteristics.
  b These groups contain a particularly large number of widely different species.

7 a An arachnid has eight legs; an insect has six.
  b Arthropods.

8 a Very thin leaves.
  b Spores.
  c Yes.
  d Conifers.
  e Yes.
  f Seeds.
  g Yes.

9 a Liverworts don't have any roots so they are not very effective at absorbing water.
  b Seeds are transmitted through the wind (using wing shapes) or carried off by animals that have eaten the fruit. This means that their offspring are not competing with them for the resources in a particular habitat.

10 The 'many legs' branch could be split into 'eight legs' (arachnids) and 'six legs' (insects). The 'needle-like leaves' results in conifers. Liverworts could be identified as having very thin leaves and living in damp conditions.

11 The foot has developed into two long feeding tentacles.

12 Invertebrates are classed in a negative way: animals without a backbone. There are far fewer species with a backbone than without and the potential for these species to differ widely is huge.

13 Sea sponges belong to the animal kingdom. They don't photosynthesise and they produce eggs and sperm. However, there is not much co-ordination between individual cells.

8   Investigating habitats

1 Sampling is taking data from random places within the habitat. The population size is often too hard to count completely and so you have to take small samples and extrapolate the data to the whole habitat.

2 Take quadrat readings along a straight line, recording all of the organisms you find. A transect is used to study how a habitat changes because of a gradual change in physical conditions – for example, across a path passing through a wood.

3 It is a diagram with rows one on top of the other. The bottom row indicates the number of producers at the bottom of a particular food chain in a habitat; the next row indicates the number of primary consumers, and so on. The width of the row represents the number it contains.

4 **a** A is a pooter; B is a pitfall trap.
  b To use the pooter you select the organism you are going to catch.
  c You can sample organisms that are not on the ground. The sampling process is much quicker than having to wait for animals to enter a trap.

5 **a** Population size is the total number of organisms; population density is the number of organisms per m^2.
  b $3 \div 100 = 0.03$ snails per m^2.
  c The environment particularly favourable to certain animals might be in small patches (e.g. dark and damp areas for woodlice).

6 **a** Animals that don't move very fast.
  b 72% (count whole and half squares of grass).
  c 28%.
  d It is hard to know where one organism begins and the other one ends.
  e Take random quadrat samples in a wide range of areas and find an average.

7 **a** Graph A; the population size is much smaller.
  b As the population of rabbits increases there is more food for the foxes so the fox population increases. However, more foxes eat more rabbits, which makes the rabbit population decrease. Then there is less food for the foxes so the

population of foxes decreases. This allows the rabbit population to increase again, and the process repeats.

9   Atoms and elements

1 No.
2 Materials are made from combinations of different elements. There is an infinite variety of combinations.
3 Metals conduct electricity; non-metals don't.
4 Mercury.
5 **a** Symbols are the same in all languages; this prevents problems in communication.
  b To distinguish between elements starting with the same letter, e.g. hydrogen (H) and helium (He).
  c The symbols are based on their original names, which have subsequently changed.
  d i Hydrogen; **ii** lithium; **iii** argon; **iv** sodium; **v** potassium; **vi** gold; **vii** mercury; **viii** antimony.
  e i He; **ii** Ca; **iii** Mg; **iv** Cl; **v** Pb; **vi** Sn.
  f Helium and chlorine are non-metals; the others are metals.
6 Iron, cobalt and nickel.
7 **a** Li, Be, B and C are solids; the others are gases.
  b Li and Be are metals; C, N, O, F and Ne are non-metals.
  c B; a metalloid.
  d N and O.
  e C.
  f It is highly reactive and combines readily with other elements.
8 **a** They are all reactive metals and their oxides are alkaline.
  b They get more reactive as seen by their behaviour in water.
  c Rubidium and caesium.
  d Alkaline earth metals; halogens; noble gases.

10 Molecules and compounds

1 The atoms in the molecule are both the same type.
2 An oxygen atom with two hydrogen atoms attached to it.
3 A carbon monoxide molecule has one carbon and one oxygen atom; a carbon dioxide molecule has one carbon and two oxygen atoms.
4 It comes from the oxygen which has formed a compound with the iron.

5 a Magnesium reacts violently with oxygen so you need to have a safety screen to protect you from potential explosions. Magnesium also burns very brightly so you have to avoid looking directly at the flame so that you don't damage your eyes.

  b Magnesium oxide.

  c Magnesium + oxygen → magnesium oxide.

  d Magnesium and oxygen atoms form a lattice structure bonded together into a crystal.

6 a Iron + sulfur → iron sulfide.

  b Fe + S → FeS.

  c One atom of iron will always react with one atom of sulfur.

  d No bonds are formed in a mixture so the iron and sulfur atoms have no effect on each other.

  e A certain number of iron atoms have a mass of 56 g. The same number of sulfur atoms have a mass of 32 g. So iron atoms are $56 \div 32 = 1.75$ times heavier than sulfur atoms.

7 a It is denser than air.

  b Sodium reacts vigorously with water which produces heat. The heat from this reaction can start the reaction between the sodium and the chlorine.

  c The flask glows very brightly.

  d The sand reduces the risk of fire.

  e Sodium + chlorine → sodium chloride.

  f Common salt.

8 a The salt in the sea water.

  b Hydrogen.

  c The water molecules.

  d Sodium chloride + water → chlorine + hydrogen + sodium hydroxide.

9 a You need to give them enough energy so that the atoms can get close enough to form bonds.

  b The reaction can produce enough heat to be self-sustaining.

11 Chemical formulae

1 H_2O and H_2S.

2 One nitrogen atom bonded to three hydrogen atoms.

3 SO_2 and HCl.

4 Two nitrogen, eight hydrogen, one sulfur and four oxygen atoms.

5 There are twice as many oxygen atoms as there are silicon atoms.

6 a C_3H_8.

  b C_5H_{12}.

7 a $CO_2 + C \rightarrow 2CO$.

  b $TiCl_4 + 4Na \rightarrow Ti + 4NaCl$.

  c $Ca(OH)_2 + 2HCl \rightarrow CaCl_2 + 2H_2O$.

  d $2H_2 + O_2 \rightarrow 2H_2O$.

  e $Fe_2O_3 + 2Al \rightarrow 2Fe + Al_2O_3$.

  f $2ZnS + 3O_2 \rightarrow 2ZnO + 2SO_2$.

  g $Fe_2O_3 + 3CO \rightarrow 2Fe + 3CO_2$.

8 a CH_3OCH_3.

  b CH_3NH_2.

  c $CH_2(OH)CH(OH)CH_2OH$.

9 $2C_2H_6 + 5O_2 \rightarrow 4CO + 6H_2O$.

10 Carbon forms four bonds; oxygen forms two bonds, nitrogen forms three bonds; hydrogen forms one bond. It is to do with the number of electrons these atoms have in their outer 'shells'.

12 Mixtures

1 It is a mixture.

2 Atoms in compounds form very specific bonds which determine the proportions that make up the compound. Mixtures don't form these bonds.

3 The compound splitting into its constituent elements. Silver chloride → silver + chlorine.

4 Impure water boils at a temperature different from 100 °C.

5 a A mixture.

  b Hydrogen is less dense than the average density of air so it floats to the top.

  c Nitrogen and oxygen.

  d Carbon dioxide and the noble gases (plus water vapour and traces of other gases).

  e Use fractional distillation.

6 a On the right-hand side in group 0.

  b Ramsey cooled air to temperatures low enough for the air to liquefy. Then he let the air boil very slowly and measured the various boiling points.

  c There were gaps in the periodic table where these elements should fit.

7 N coolant, fertilisers; O medicine, welding, rocket fuel; Ne lighting; He meteorological balloons; Kr bright lights; Xe even brighter lights.

8 a Lead is a poisonous material and too dangerous to use in schools.

  b 250 °C.

  c The tin becomes more concentrated.

d Approximately 180 °C.

e It is lower than both melting points.

f It remains molten over a wide range of temperatures so it is easier to work with before it completely freezes.

9 Amalgam: mixture of metal and mercury; alloy: mixture of metals; gel: mixture of solid particles in a liquid; aerosol: mixture of solid or liquid particles in a gas.

10 The particles of the other element get in the way of the bonds being formed.

13 Weathering of rocks

1 Minerals are materials with a crystalline structure that are the building blocks of rock.

2 All of them are, apart from diamond which is a mineral, and peat which is made from plant material.

3 Weathering is the breaking up of rocks. Erosion is the wearing away of rocks.

4 Physical weathering is the breaking up of rock using force; chemical weathering uses chemical reactions.

5 a It expands.

b Water enters the rock and then expands when it freezes, forcing the rock apart.

c A climate where the temperature frequently fluctuates above and below 0 °C.

6 a 25 cm³.

b 3 cm³, assuming that all of the missing water has entered the chalk rather than evaporated.

c $(3 \div 25) \times 100 = 12\%$.

d The chalk.

e Granite is made from interlocking grains, but chalk has lots of gaps in it.

f Granite; chalk would allow the water to leak out.

7 a The rocks expand and contract in the hot and cold temperatures. This continued cycle weakens them and they break apart.

b Plant life (e.g. tree roots) can force the stones apart. This is called biological weathering.

8 a Rain (or snow) passing through the atmosphere.

b $H_2O + CO_2 \rightarrow H_2CO_3$.

c Calcium carbonate.

d The limestone reacts with the carbonic acid and dissolves in the water. The water then flows away, taking the limestone with it.

e Sulfur dioxide can dissolve in water to produce sulfuric acid. This is a stronger acid than carbonic acid and reacts with the limestone much more quickly.

9 Cave formations are formed due to the erosion of limestone. Stalagmites and stalactites come from the reverse of the reaction: calcium hydrogen carbonate back into calcium carbonate.

10 Every time the water freezes, cracks get wider and new cracks are formed. This allows more water in when the process repeats, which can obviously cause even more damage. Eventually the rock is so weakened due to the number of cracks that it breaks apart.

11 They have cooled down and contracted. The contraction forces have cracked the rock.

14 Sedimentary layers

1 It comprises small particles of weathered rock and other materials carried by rivers and streams.

2 As geological processes change, the source of the sediment falling on a particular sea bed changes, leading to a different layer.

3 The ocean floors are the lowest regions of the Earth's surface.

4 a The gradient of the river is steeper.

b They flow faster.

c They settle on the river bed.

d When the river is flooding or moving very quickly due to rainy weather.

e They get weathered and eroded.

f They have been in the river for longer, and the river flows more slowly nearer the sea so only the small particles can be carried.

5 a The slower water can't carry the bigger rock fragments.

b The outside of the bend.

c The build up of sediment and erosion can eventually change the direction of the river.

6 a Glaciers: they can carry much bigger fragments of rock than rivers.

b The wind carries sediment.

7 Sedimentary rock builds up over time. Therefore the lower layers were deposited earlier and will contain earlier fossils.

8 a It dissolves in water.

b The water gets trapped in a lake and evaporates.

c Since the salt hasn't dissolved, there can't be any water.

9 a Sea creatures use the calcium in the water to produce their shells which are obviously insoluble. When they die, they sink to the bottom of the sea.
  b Calcium carbonate (limestone).
10 You could see how animals changed over time and how certain features evolved.
11 Iridium isn't common in the Earth's crust but it is common in meteorites. This is evidence that the dinosaurs were wiped out by a meteorite impact.
12 Plant material in swamps couldn't be decomposed quickly enough by bacteria before they formed a sediment of peat. This eventually became coal. Oil and gas comes from the sediment caused by the plankton in the sea. Oil companies look for layers of porous rock covered by layers of non-porous rock which could be trapping the oil.

15 Types of rock

1 Sedimentary and possibly metamorphic.
2 All three types (even metamorphic rock can change into a new type of metamorphic rock).
3 High temperatures and pressures.
4 They have been compacted together with great forces and so they are held together more strongly.
5 a Sedimentary.
  b They are getting squashed into an interlocking structure.
  c Water leaks into the sandstone, evaporates and deposits its minerals.
  d They are produced in a very similar way to the matrix, except that there is room for the crystals to grow larger.
6 a A large earthquake might have folded the rocks.
  b Pressure and heat would have been created in this process.
  c The mineral crystals within the rock alter their structure at different temperatures and pressures (e.g. graphite and diamond). This alters the properties of the rock.
7 a They all contain calcium carbonate.
  b The proportion of calcium carbonate varies.
8 a Marble.
  b It is non-porous and can be split into flat layers.
  c They get smaller and form layers.
  d They have been squashed with the rocks.
  e Minerals are formed from different combinations of atoms bonding together. The same atoms are still there but they have bonded together differently.

9 a The freezing of molten rock.
  b Intrusive igneous rock is formed below the Earth's surface; extrusive igneous rock is formed above the surface.
10 a Igneous.
   b Metamorphic.
   c Igneous.
   d Sedimentary.
   e Sedimentary.
   f Metamorphic.
   g Igneous.
   h Metamorphic.
   i Igneous.
11 Meteoritic rock.
12 Silicon and oxygen are the most abundant elements in the Earth's crust.
13 Small regions are due to localised effects such as heating caused by magma intrusions; large regions are due to large-scale effects such as boundaries between tectonic plates.

16 The rock cycle

1 Igneous rocks are weathered and eroded. The sediment is transported to the ocean floor where it eventually changes into sedimentary rock.
2 Magma.
3 High temperatures and high pressures.
4 They are mixtures of lots of different minerals.
5 a The molecules /particles gradually slow down and bond together in regular patterns as the magma cools.
  b Igneous rock.
  c The larger the crystals, the slower the cooling process.
  d Melt some very pure silicon and let it solidify very slowly.
6 a A new layer of igneous rock is formed every time the volcano erupts.
  b Surrounding the regions where lava flows, especially lower down.
7 a Intrusive rocks form underground and so cool down much more slowly.
  b It is less dense than water.
  c It has cooled down so quickly that it has lots of air holes.
8 a Basalt.
  b Granite and rhyolite are silica rich; gabbro and basalt are iron rich (iron is denser).

c Gabbro is found in oceanic crust (since it is denser); granite is found in continental crust.

9 a Metamorphic.
  b Weathering, erosion and transportation.
  c Sediment.
  d Sedimentary rock.
  e Magma.
  f Uplift.

17 Heat and temperature

1 Temperature.
2 Have three bowls of water: one hot, one cold, the other one warm. Place your left hand in the hot bowl and your right hand in the cold bowl. Once your hands have got used to the temperatures, quickly put both hands in the warm bowl.
3 They move because they have some kinetic energy but they are held in place by the bonds between them.
4 The joule (J).
5 a Your hand.
  b From your hand to the table.
  c From your hand to the spoon.
  d Metals are better conductors of heat.
  e Heat is transferring away more quickly, which is the same effect as touching a cold object.
  f No.
  g Objects that are at the same temperature can feel at different temperatures. Therefore to make sense of this quantity you need to design instruments to measure it properly. For instruments to give a value for the temperature, you need a scale to base this value on.
6 a A lighted match.
  b A warm mug of coffee; more energy has gone into warming the coffee up than could be supplied by a lighted match.
7 a 0 °C.
  b Some of the water would freeze into ice.
  c All of the water will have frozen.
  d All of the ice will have melted.
  e Boiling water consists of liquid and gas at the same temperature.
  f Place the thermometer in the ice/water mix and mark 0 °C, then place the thermometer in boiling water and mark 100 °C. Then divide the scale into 100 equal parts.

8 a The particles move slower when it is cold.
  b i They vibrate faster; ii they split apart from each other; iii they move around faster.
  c The particles don't move any faster at this point since the energy goes into breaking the bonds.
  d A similar horizontal line will appear higher up as the paraffin boils.
9 It comes from the bonds being made (particles lose potential energy).
10 The rate that heat is transferred depends on the temperature difference. When the coffee is hot, lots of heat is being emitted so it cools down quicker than when it is cold.
11 Lots of glass containers of different densities float in some water. The density of the water changes with temperature and this can be observed by certain glass containers sinking.

18 Heat transfer

1 It is a process that impedes heat transfer.
2 The holes contain trapped air, which is a good insulator.
3 It reduces heat transfer in both directions. Hot things are kept hot by reducing heat transfer out of the flask. Cold things are kept cold by reducing heat transfer into the flask.
4 The material has to move. Solids can't do this.
5 a Kinetic energy.
  b Particles at the hot end have more kinetic energy than those at the cold end.
  c All of the particles have the same kinetic energy (on average).
  d The particles have collided with each other, passing on their kinetic energy.
6 a It stops the ice floating to the top.
  b Water is a very poor conductor of heat.
  c The heat energy would transfer through the copper to the bottom.
7 The particles are closer together and collide with each other more frequently.
8 a The particles move more vigorously and take up more space.
  b Its density gets less and the upthrust force becomes greater than its weight.
9 a A convection current is set up by the candle. The smoke moves with the falling colder air.
  b The smoke rises.
  c Convection.

10 Conduction and convection need particles. Space is a vacuum so heat transfer from the Sun can't be from these two methods.
11 They have free electrons which can move easily through the metal, colliding as they go.
12 They trap a layer of air, stopping it from convecting. Air is a very poor conductor of heat.
13 They emit less heat radiation than black surfaces.
14 It goes from the warm back of the fridge into the room.

19 Magnetism

1 Cobalt, nickel and iron oxide are magnetic; the other materials aren't.
2 N and S attract; N and N repel; S and S repel.
3 It points due north if suspended from a piece of string.
4 A magnet has N and S poles; a magnetic material is simply attracted to a pole of a magnet.
5 It is a material that reduces the magnetic field. Surround the spaceship with a magnetic material.
6 Magnets: A, C, D; magnetic materials: B, E; not magnetic: F.
7 a A is slightly magnetised; B is fully magnetised; C is unmagnetised.
  b Once all the domains point the same way, you can't make the effect any stronger.
  c It makes the domains jiggle about and point in random directions again.
8 a It is a region where a magnetic force acts.
  b Towards the S pole.
  c They are closest together.
  d It gets weaker.
  e The S pole of the magnet (since N poles will be attracted to it).
  f It is the same shape as that for a bar magnet with the field lines looping away from the geographical south pole around the Earth to enter the surface of the Earth at the geographical north pole. (In reality the magnetic poles are at a small angle to the geographic poles.)
9 A is a wire wound in a solenoid (spring) shape; B is produced by a straight wire.
10 The Earth's magnetic field exerts a weak force on the domains which makes them line up if gently tapped.
11 The domains in the iron line up with the weak field. Each domain produces a little magnetic field which adds to the total effect.

20 Using magnetism

1 A solenoid of wire and an iron core.
2 Greater current and more turns of wire.
3 Reverse the direction of the current.
4 It quickly loses its magnetism.
5 a An a.c. current continually swaps direction; a d.c. current always goes the same way.
  b It is changing direction.
  c Clamp the spring blade at one end above the electromagnet. The blade springs up when the magnet is off and down when the magnet is on. Therefore the blade vibrates up and down.
  d The paper clip is attracted both to N and S poles. Therefore it doesn't matter if the poles keep swapping.
6 a It is an electromagnetic switch. It is used to allow circuits with a low current to control circuits with high currents.
  b If the electromagnet is on, the switch is pulled down and closes the circuit; if the electromagnet is off the spring pulls the switch open again.
7 a When the current gets too high, the electromagnet becomes strong enough to pull the switch open against the pull of the spring.
  b The electromagnet would no longer attract the switch and it would close again. The switch needs to be permanently open until the fault is fixed.
8 a It switches on.
  b The electromagnet attracts the armature towards it.
  c The contacts are separated, which breaks the circuit.
  d It is lifted away from the gong by the spring.
  e The contacts touch again.
  f The situation is back to how it was in part **a** and the process repeats.
9 Soft magnetic materials lose their magnetism at room temperature; hard materials don't. An electromagnet using steel (a hard magnetic material) would be permanently on, even if the current was switched off.
10 High currents heat up wires. Eventually the copper wire melts and the electromagnet stops working. Superconducting wires don't heat up when they carry large currents.
11 Half of the domains will point one way and half will point in the opposite way, thereby balancing their magnetic fields.

21 Light and reflection

1 The speed of light.
2 Both let light through but you can see objects clearly through transparent material.
3 Opaque materials form shadows, since they don't let any light through.
4 Behind it.
5 a Don't look directly into it or at its reflections. Put a warning sign that you are using it outside the door.
 b The light has to enter your eye.
 c The light reflected off the liquid droplets of deodorant into their eyes.
 d A straight line.
6 a You see the objects inside the shop and also your reflection.
 b You don't see any reflections.
 c You would see the insides of the shop more brightly.
7 a

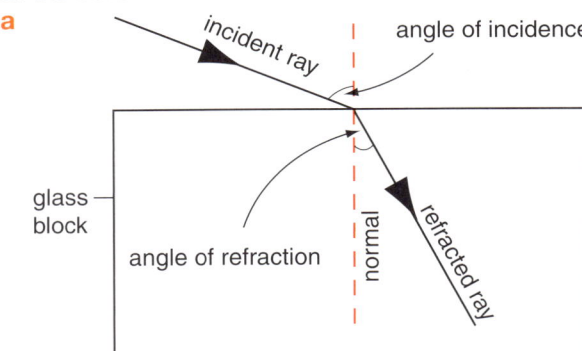

 b They are always equal.
 c 120°.
8 a 20 cm.
 b Left and right are swapped. An inverted image would be upside down as well.
 c CHICK is reflected but it is symmetrical so it looks the same.
9 a 180°; they are like a single, flat mirror.
 b 7.
 c An infinite number.
 d Each image gets slightly dimmer since the mirror absorbs energy. Eventually the images will become too dim (and too far away) to see.
10 You can't capture it on a screen. Light seems to be coming from it but doesn't actually.

11 3×10^8 m/s. A light-year is the distance that light travels in a year.

22 Refraction and colour

1 It is the changing of direction of light due to a change in speed.
2 Dispersion.
3 Primary colours are pure colours. Secondary colours are equal mixtures of two primary colours.
4 The dye in the jeans reflects blue light but absorbs all the other colours.
5 a

 b It also reflects a little.
 c It slows down.
 d The angle of refraction is smaller than the angle of incidence.
 e The ray is going along a normal line (they are both at 90°).
6 The rays leaving the surface of the pool bend outwards and look as though they have come from higher up than the bottom.
7 a Different colours travel at different speeds and so refract by different amounts.
 b The visible spectrum.
 c He masked off all of the other colours apart from green and made the light go through a second prism. There was no further dispersion.
8 The middle is white; red and green give yellow; red and blue give magenta; blue and green give cyan.
9 They absorb the green light and reflect the blue light.
10 Red: red, black, black, red, black, red.

 Blue: black, blue, black, black, blue, blue.

 Green: black, black, green, green, green, black.

 Yellow: red, black, green, yellow, green, red.

 Cyan: black, blue, green, green, cyan, blue.

11 Compound yellow is red and green light. Pure yellow is the colour produced in the visible spectrum.

12 Black.

13 Our eyes detect red, green and blue light only (with some overlap). Pure yellow light equally stimulates the red and green cells since this colour lies between red and green in the visible spectrum. Another way of stimulating these cells in the same way is to shine equal amounts of red and green light.

23 Sound waves

1 They are carried by vibrating particles.

2 The speed of sound is fastest in solids and slowest in gases.

3 It is the number of vibrations per second. The unit is hertz (Hz).

4 It is bigger.

5 a They vibrate.
  b Make the string shorter or tighter.
  c They have different thicknesses.

6 a A.
  b B and C.
  c Very loud and low.
  d A and B.
  e C is louder than B.
  f The amplitude would decrease. Increase the amplification of the microphone (or the volts/division setting on the oscilloscope).

7 a They have the same amplitude and same frequency.
  b Their shapes would be different.

8 a Vibrating particles of water collide with the rubber sheet making it vibrate. The sheet collides with air, making the air particles vibrate, and these collide with each other making the vibrations pass along the tube.
  b It focuses the energy into a smaller space.
  c Backwards and forwards (rather than up and down).
  d The sound waves reflect at the surface of the water back into the water, so hardly any energy is transmitted into the air.

9 a The particles in solids are held closer so the vibrations can pass along more quickly.
  b The railway lines transmit the sound from a long distance away.
  c Water doesn't absorb sound energy as much as air does.

  d The seismic waves are the same as the sound waves.

10 The sound reflects from your hands to go just in one direction rather than in all directions.

11 Our ears are more sensitive at these frequencies, so they sound louder even though they aren't. Babies' ears are very sensitive at higher frequencies.

24 Hearing sound

1 20 Hz to 20 000 Hz.

2 The high end of the range gets less.

3 The decibel scale.

4 a Energy gets funnelled in the outer ear and becomes more intense. It gets converted into mechanical energy at the eardrum and is transmitted through the ossicles. The vibration of the stirrup in the oval window allows the mechanical energy to pass to the fluid in the cochlea. Finally the mechanical energy of the fluid gets transformed into electrical energy in the auditory nerve.
  b It makes the sound more intense and it helps in sensing the direction of the sound.
  c Since the amplitude of vibration is bigger more energy is transferred to the fluid in the cochea.
  d It would limit the energy reaching the auditory nerve.
  e Fluid transmits sound energy quickly and efficiently.
  f It allows the membrane surrounding the auditory nerve to have a large surface area.

5 a These vibrations can travel directly to the fluid in the cochlea, by-passing the damaged ear.
  b The auditory nerve.
  c A damaged ear will respond by different amounts to different frequencies. The hearing aid needs to balance all of these frequencies back to normal levels again.

6 a It is the quietest sound you can hear.
  b Their hearing is impaired since they can only just hear a sound that is louder than 40 dB.

7 a 3000 Hz.
  b Alarms ring at this value so that they are easily heard.
  c The whole graph will move upwards and the higher frequency end will move up still further.